Vasconcellos, J.
The War Lords

THE WAR
LORDS

THE WAR LORDS

Measuring **STRATEGY** and **TACTICS** for
COMPETITIVE ADVANTAGE in **BUSINESS**

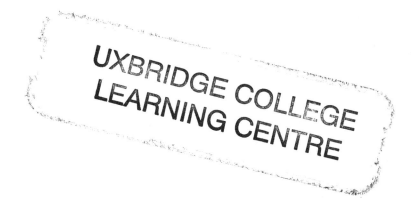

JORGE VASCONCELLOS E SÁ

**KOGAN
PAGE**

YOURS TO HAVE AND TO HOLD
BUT NOT TO COPY

First published in English in 1999

Kogan Page Limited
120 Pentonville Road
London N1 9JN
UK

Kogan Page Limited
163 Central Avenue, Suite 4
Dover
NH 03820
USA

British Library Cataloguing in Publication Data
A CIP record for this book is available from the British Library.
ISBN 0 7494 2824 4

Typeset by Patrick Armstrong, Book Production Services
Printed and bound by Biddles Ltd, Guildford and King's Lynn

To my wife

Contents

About the author

Jorge Vasconcellos e Sá has a PhD in Business Administration from Columbia University in New York. At present he is a professor at the Technical and Modern Universities. He has published more than 20 articles in international magazines, such as *Strategic Management Journal*, *European Management Journal*, *Long Range Planning*, *Industrial Marketing Management* and *Business and European Marketing Journal*.

Professor Vasconcellos has addressed conferences and given seminars at various European universities including London Business School, IESE (Navarra University, Spain), Glasgow Business School, ESSEC (France) and ESSAM.

As a private consultant and teacher in executive programmes he has worked for companies such as Shell, Unisys, IBM, Price Waterhouse, Klynveld Peat Main Goerdeler, Glaxo, British Petroleum, Dum & Bradstreet and Makro (Metro Group).

In public administration he has been a consultant to ministries of industry, finance, transport, agriculture, economic planning, local administration and state modernization. He has also worked as a private consultant for the European Union Central Commission, the International Labour Organization and the Phare and Tacis programmes.

In 1997 Jorge Vasconcellos e Sá earned the Jean Monnet Chair, the high European academic award.

A note to the reader:
A book on strategic
management with a war title?

This is a book about *strategic management*; that is, *strategy within business administration*. It is not about war. So, why the title? And why dedicate the first chapter to military warfare?

The title *The Warlords* comes from the fact that economics is today what Clausewitz (one of the great interpreters of Napoleon) once said of war: *the continuation of politics by other means*. Indeed, two centuries after Clausewitz wrote, nations are increasingly promoting their national interests through economic might instead of warfare. They support firms connected to or controlled by their citizens (as managers, shareholders or both); and they aim at conquering larger shares of markets.[1]

Why? Because economic power influences political power. As the Russian proverb goes: he whose bread I eat, his the song I sing. Or as it is said in the USA: when money talks, people listen. Thus entrepreneurs and managers are the true warlords of the 21st century.

Why then dedicate the opening chapter to military warfare (Hannibal's campaign against the Romans: 218–216 BC)? Because military warfare was the field which *pioneered* the concept of strategy, and Hannibal's campaign is a good example of what strategy is *and is not*, as well as of its relation with tactics. As will be shown, the military concept of strategy – where to combat the enemy (in contrast to tactics, which concerns how to do it) – has a a *direct* and very *useful* application in business administration. Strategy first clarifies and, second, makes things much easier in terms of day-to-day implementation. Other advantages, though less important, follow: the original concept of the word is respected and communication simplified; one has one word, one concept (instead of one word, two concepts: one in military warfare and another in business administration).

Then, from the example of Hannibal's campaign in Chapter 1 and from Chapter 2 to the end, this book first indicates *how to make a strategic plan* and then *how to measure strategy*: by *quantifying*, *qualifying* and *synthesizing* it. This is an important task indeed, since *strategists are like surgeons: their mistakes are generally deadly.*

Preface

Thucydides (460–395 BC) mentioned that peace was nothing more than a brief armistice in a permanent state of war. However, in business there are no armistices; the war is continuous.

As war is a stage of uncertainties (Carl von Clausewitz said, 'No other human activity is so influenced by luck as war'), throughout time people have tried to define the principles which, when followed, ensure success and victory.

The Romans believed that *audaces fortuna juvat* (luck favours the bold), while for Wellington, 'Defence is the means by which the gods of war allow men to multiply in number.' For Napoleon Bonaparte, 'God protects the large battalions', but Alexander the Great proved the opposite when one after another in Issus and Gaugamela he defeated the Persian armies which greatly outnumbered his troops.

On what side are the gods of war? On the side of boldness or defence? On the side of the large armies or the swiftness and mobility of troops? What laws, what principles must be used to design a strategy and formulate a plan of war in business?

With the passage of time, history has shown that the war gods are not on the side of the bold, nor the cautious, nor the large battalions, nor the most mobile armies, but are on the side of those who follow certain principles of strategy, which have remained constant throughout time, which is the same as saying that God helps those who help themselves.

These principles are dealt with throughout this book, starting with a military war in the 3rd century BC and ending with the contemporary war in business – a journey lasting more than two thousand years in which, as the writer of Ecclesiastes said, 'There is no new thing under the sun.' Or, as Napoleon once said, *'I have fought sixty battles and I learned nothing I did not know in the beginning.'*

Preface

1

Hannibal in Cannae

The Battle of Cannae (painting by Heinz Zander, 1973, Dresden Museum)

INTRODUCTION

In this chapter, we will define the concepts of strategy and tactics, in simple but rigorous terms. Since neither concept was invented by business administration (in contrast to other concepts such as segmentation, critical success factors, etc) it makes good sense first to go to the field which pioneered the concepts (military warfare) and, second, to see how to apply these concepts to business administration.

For this purpose, the campaign of Hannibal in the second war between Rome and Carthage was selected; because of its importance (the Battle of Cannae was one of the greatest Roman disasters ever) and because this campaign illustrated clearly the distinction between strategy and tactics. Strategy refers to *where* to combat the enemy (competition); tactics *how* to do it.

The advantages of defining strategy in such a way are threefold. First, it respects the original idea behind the concept. Second, communication becomes simpler, since we now have one word – one idea – instead of the same word meaning two different ideas: one in military affairs, the other in business administration. Third, the military concept of strategy can be applied to business administration in a very useful way, making a clear-cut distinction between which decisions are strategic and which are tactical.

Respect, *simplicity* and *utility* make the military concept of strategy (*where* to combat the enemy) a very powerful instrument, as we shall see. Let us then start with Hannibal in 218 BC.

> *The gods did not give all the qualities to just one man. Hannibal, you know how to win a battle but you do not know how to exploit a victory.*
>
> MAHARBAL, CAVALRY COMMANDER AFTER THE BATTLE OF CANNAE (216 BC) AND CONFRONTED WITH HANNIBAL'S REFUSAL TO MARCH ON ROME, 70 KILOMETRES AWAY.

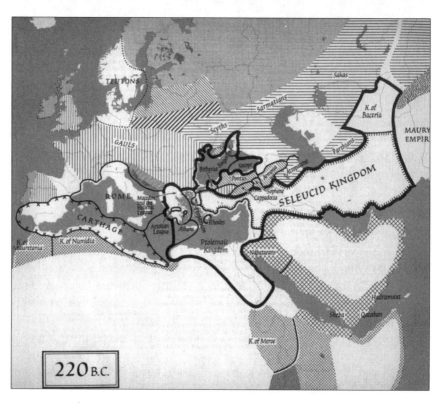

Figure 1.1 The Ancient World in Hannibal's time

As a result of the Carthaginian attack on Saguntum, an Iberian city under the protection of Rome, war was declared on Carthage in 218 BC. Thus began the Second Punic War.

The political geography of the world at that time was as is shown in Figure 1.1. Carthage not only controlled a large part of North Africa but also the southern part of the Iberian Peninsula. Hannibal had his headquarters in Cartagena, near the present-day city of Valencia.

Hannibal had four strategic alternatives (see Figure 1.2). The first was to remain in the Iberian Peninsula and await the disembarkation of the Roman fleet which had dominated the western Mediterranean since the First Punic War. Second, a possible alternative was to embark his army and fight the Roman fleet at sea. A third alternative was to try and cross the Mediterranean and fortify Carthage, in North Africa, protecting it from a direct attack by Rome. Finally, the fourth possibility was to cross the Pyrenees and the Alps, emerging in the Po Valley in north Italy. As is well known, Hannibal opted for this alternative, glorified in Hans Baumann's romance, *Ich Zog mit Annibal*.

After a 900 kilometre journey, Hannibal descended the Alps and defeated three Roman armies in a row. The first two victories occurred in the Po Valley, near the Ticino and Trebia rivers and the third was a year later after crossing the Apennines near Lake Trasimene.

The Romans reacted with their usual force against Hannibal and sent 16 legions – about 80,000 infantry and 6,000 cavalry – commanded by Consuls Lucius Paulus and Caius Varro. The Carthaginian army had

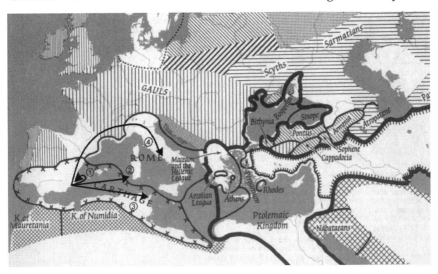

Figure 1.2 Hannibal's alternative strategies in the Second Punic War

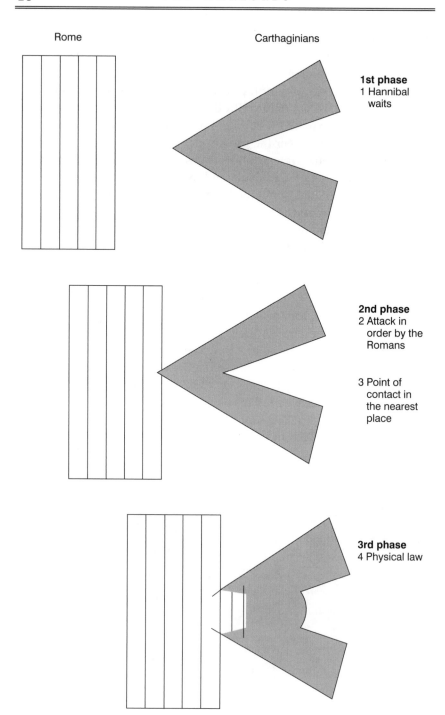

Figure 1.3 The first three phases of the Battle of Cannae

about half the number of the Roman troops – 10,000 cavalry (2,000 Numidians and 8,000 Moors) and infantry of little more than 30,000, made up of Libyans, Gauls, Iberians and mercenaries from Carthage.

Hannibal waited for the Roman army in Cannae. We have first-hand information of what happened afterwards from Sosilo, the Greek historian of Hannibal, and Silenos's commentaries about the war, translated into Latin by Lucius Coelius Antipater. Although his army was smaller, Hannibal had two pieces of very valuable information about the enemy. The first referred to the Roman way of making war: the basic unit was the legion of 3,600 heavy infantry soldiers, another 1,200 more lightly armed men and 300 horsemen, totalling about 5,000. They always moved systematically in blocks of closed lines and the cavalry was placed on the wings. They were famous for their discipline and rigour of movements during the battles.[1]

The second piece of valuable information possessed by Hannibal concerned the state of his enemy's mind. After a year of delaying tactics – resulting from three defeats by the Roman General Fabius who was therefore given the nickname of *cunctator* (the delayer) by Roman public opinion – action was demanded. It should be added that the consuls Paulus and Varro relied on their superior numbers.[2] Hannibal was aware of this.

Using the Roman state of mind to his advantage, Hannibal placed his army as shown in Figure 1.3 and ordered it to wait. The centre was the weakest for three reasons. It had fewer lines of men, was made up of locally recruited troops from Gaul and Iberia, and these were more lightly armed. The wings, on the contrary, were the stronger part of the Carthaginian army as they had a greater number of lines and the elite, better trained and best armed troops were concentrated there: the mercenaries from Carthage and the cavalry under the command of Maharbal.

The battle started when Hannibal sent his cavalry in to attack the Roman cavalry on both wings of their army. The higher number (10,000 against 6,000) and the superior skill of Hannibal's Moorish, Numidian and Gallic horsemen decided the battle.[3] However, the loss of the cavalry did not worry Varro too much as he believed in the essential strength of the Roman army which was its infantry, where he still had great superiority of numbers (74,000 against 40,000). So he gave the order for his army to advance.

The second phase of the battle started, shown in Figure 1.3. The Roman army moved in order, like an immense machine with the contact between the two armies occurring in the place nearest between them (see Figure 1.3).

When two elements collide, the weakest gives way. At this time the

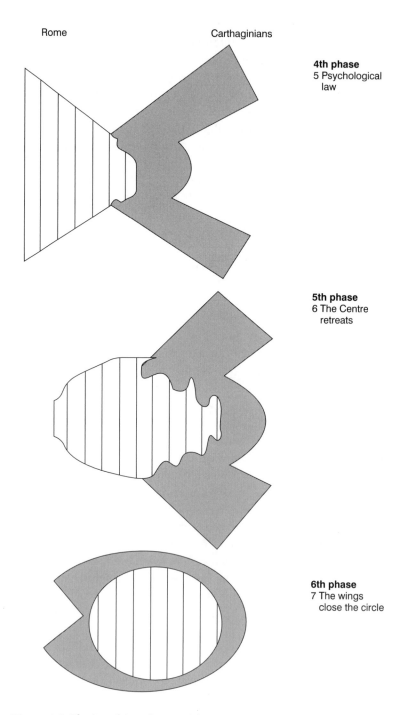

Figure 1.4 The last three phases of the Battle of Cannae

weakest meant: first, fewer lines of men; second, lighter arms and, third, less training. It was the centre of the Carthaginian force. To avoid this being breached, Hannibal gave the order to retreat, and thus the third stage of the battle started.

At this moment a psychological law came into operation, of which Hannibal – with his military experience obtained first of all in the shadow of his father Amilcar and later on from his brother-in-law Asdrubal – was well aware. In the heat of the battle the Roman legionaries on the wings continued to march in order, but still had not come into contact with the enemy. However, looking at the centre of their army, they could see that not only was it engaged with the Carthaginian army but also it was obliged to give way. In the heat of the battle, the natural tendency is for the legionaries to converge on the centre of the enemy army.[4] That is what they did and Hannibal was counting on it. Then the fourth phase of the battle began (see Figure 1.4).

Hannibal gave the order for his centre to retreat even further, first, to avoid it being broken under the added pressure of the legionaries and, second, to advance the centre of the battle nearer to the Carthaginian wings (5th phase in Figure 1.4). Once that was done, Hannibal simply ordered his wings to contain the cavalry and the elite of his infantry circled the Romans (see 6th phase in Figure 1.4).

The Romans, encircled and unable to manoeuvre, suffered 48,000 dead and 100,000 prisoners. A contingent of 14,000 managed to open a breach and escape between the centre of the Carthaginian army and one of its flanks.[5]

It was *the greatest disaster in the military history of Rome until Arausio*, a century later (103 AD). Then Quinto Servilio Cipian and Malio Maximo – due to rivalry among themselves, instead of joining forces and forming a powerful army of 17 legions (90 men) – decided to face the Germanos (as an emigration of Cimbrians and Teutonics coming from present-day Denmark was then called) separately. Rome was successively defeated with two armies separated by 20 miles and only 13 of the 90,000 legionaries survived.

Historians have continually debated, even until now, whether Hannibal did not commit the cardinal mistake of his life by not marching on Rome (70 kilometres away), after his total victory. Although he may have regretted this decision later, at that time Hannibal did not have enough equipment for the siege and wagered more on the political consequences at home of the defeat of Rome.[6]

As a result of this victory and after having pursued the fugitives of the Roman army, in Hannibal's presence Marharbal upheld that he should be allowed to go at the front of cavalry in the direction of Rome and 'The Romans will know we have arrived before being aware we were on the way.' Confronted with Hannibal's refusal, with the argument that he needed time to think, Maharbal retorted that the gods had not given all the qualities to just one man, as he, Hannibal, knew how to win a battle but did not know how to exploit a victory.

This was the first explicit reference to the concepts of strong and weak points of an entity (person, company, country).[7] These concepts are crucial in the first large model of strategy in the area of business, developed in the 1950s at Harvard by Learned, Christensen and Andrews. According to them, the performance of an entity in a certain activity depends on the fact that the strong points of the former are equal to the critical factors of success of the second.

However that may be, in the third book of the *History of the World*, Polibio and then Tito Livio guaranteed a special place for the Battle of Cannae in the history of military art and… tactics.[8] In fact all the grouping of the forces and their movements during the battle are linked to *tactics* and not *strategy*, as defined by the military forces. Both concepts have a simple, direct and very useful similarity in the business area.[9] This is the theme of the next chapter.

2

Strategy and tactics

Sun Tzu teaches King Ho-lü's concubines

INTRODUCTION

This chapter will *apply to business administration* the concepts of strategy and tactics illustrated in the previous chapter by Hannibal's campaign. It will define some *fundamental* aspects of the use of the concept of strategy, such as:

- the basic *criteria* on which a strategy should be selected for any institution;
- the *unit of analysis* of strategy which in case of demand is the market segment, and in the case of supply is the strategic group;
- the *impact* of modifications of strategy on the alterations of tactics;
- *how to define a market segment* (one must indicate the product, geographical area, the need and the client);
- the *difference* between current strategy and future strategy;

- the *organization objective(s)* prior to defining a strategy;
- the concept of *strategic movement*;
- the *relation* between strategy and other concepts such as global service;
- how to use the concept of *strategic groups* to make inferences regarding the synergy and attractiveness of industries;
- examples of strategic and tactical *decisions*.

Strategic decisions are broken down into their *three essential elements*:

1   choice of *geographical area* of activity for the company (eg Portugal, Catalonia, the United States, Canada);

2   within a geographical area the choice of *industry* (eg textiles, footwear, hotel, wine, paper pulp);

3   choice of the *segment(s)* in which the company will focus within each industry and within each geographical area. For example, in textiles and garments a firm can choose from among hats, sports clothes, decorative materials, T-shirts, polo necks and so on.

> *The best battle plan is to win it beforehand through strategy.*
> SUN TZU
>
> *All men can see the tactics I use to conquer, but no one can foresee the strategy on which my victory is based.*
> SUN TZU

THE CONCEPTS OF STRATEGY AND TACTICS

Hannibal's campaign clearly illustrates the difference between strategy and tactics.[1] In precisely the same way as soldiers use the terms, *strategy* is the decision referring to the place, time and conditions of the battle, while *tactics* are connected with the grouping and movements of the forces during the battles (cavalry, infantry, artillery, etc). That is, strategy is decided prior to the battle but tactics are used during the battle. Strategy refers to *where* to fight the enemy (competition), tactics *how* to do it. Both are important and necessary conditions for victory, but they are well-defined and distinct from one another.

In Hannibal's campaign, his strategic decision is his choice between four alternatives: to stay *where* he was and await the Roman disembarkation in Iberia (maintenance), retreat to North Africa, fight the Roman fleet on the Mediterranean Sea or fight in Italy. After he opted for this last strategic alternative, his tactical decisions are connected with *how* Hannibal fought the successive armies sent by Rome. In Cannae in one way, in the Battle of Ticino in another, in Trebia in yet another, and so on. Victory in a military campaign (business) depends on both things, but they are conceptually different. Both good strategy and good tactics are necessary conditions; one of them alone is insufficient.

The distinction between strategy and tactics is also illustrated by Marshal Joffre, a French First World War hero. On one occasion he was asked to define strategy in simple terms. He went to a blackboard, drew an X somewhere on it and said: 'Strategy is the decision to fight here and not there, or there.' Tactics (after having made that decision) is how to fight in that place (the grouping and movement of the forces during the battle) – see Figure 2.1. As Karl von Clausewitz, one of Napoleon's great interpreters, said briefly, 'Strategy is where you are and with what strength.'[2]

Having arrived here there are some important aspects to analyse. First of all, why use the concepts of military strategy and tactics in business? Second, why are the concepts of strategy and tactics superior to the other concepts of strategy found in business literature, ie strategy as being that which is important and strategy as applying to the long term? Finally, how should these concepts of strategy and tactics of military art transplant in detail to business, and what are the implications of this? Let us consider each one of these points.

Figure 2.1 The concept of strategy according to Marshal Joffre

SUPERIORITY OF CONCEPT

As mentioned in the last chapter, there are three reasons for using the concept of military strategy in business: respect, simplicity and utility. There should be respect for the earliest concept of a word, originally developed in another area of knowledge. In fact, unlike some other words and concepts used in the world of business, the word 'strategy' was not invented by students of management (see Table 2.1). Therefore, before we start to give certain meanings to the word, it makes sense to ask ourselves what it meant in the area in which it was originally developed.[3] Another meaning should only be given to a word or phrase used in the area of business if it brings some added advantage. That is not the case with 'strategy'.

The second advantage of respecting the original concept of the word 'strategy' is simplicity in the language. Communication is facilitated whenever a word has only one single meaning. Facility of communication results from a one-to-one relationship between word and concept. Therefore when hearing the word 'strategy', the listener immediately associates this with a sole idea (where) and does not need to ask anything more, nor does the speaker have to give any additional explanation about the meaning of the word.

Finally, the concept that strategy corresponds to where (by contrast, tactics corresponds to how) is more useful than other ways in which it has been used in business literature; for example, using 'strategy' to refer to

Table 2.1 Concepts used in management

Originating in Management	Originating from Other Areas of Knowledge
1. Critical factors of success 2. Segmentation 3. Fit between Strategy and Structure 4. Life cycle of the product 5. Unit of strategic business 6. Strategic group	
	1. Optimization 2. One-to-one relationship 3. Job involvement 4. Satisfaction (in the job) 5. Strength 6. Strategy

Table 2.2 Strategy and tactics

2. 2. 1	Strategy	Tactics
Where	Yes	
How		Yes

2. 2. 2	Strategy	Tactics
Where	Geographical area(s) Industry(ies) Segment(s)	
How (Functional departments)		Financial management Accounting Personnel management Marketing Management informations systems Production Organization and control

important decisions (and 'tactics' for the remainder), or 'strategy' referring to the long term and 'tactics' to the short term.

In fact, using the military and original definition two types of decisions can be clearly distinguished: those which involve the strategic choice of *where* the business will be (to invoice, to acquire clients), including decisions referring to the *geographical areas, industries* and *segments,* and those which are the tactical decisions then needed, such as publicity, how to establish communication channels, how to organize the analytical accounts, which suppliers to choose, what machines to buy, etc. Thus tactical decisions in business include everything referring to the functional departments: marketing, accounts, production, etc – see Table 2.2. *If strategy is that which is important and tactics what is unimportant,* companies would only have strategic planning departments and no functional departments (finance, personnel, marketing, etc). Why waste time and money on what is unimportant? Similarly in the curriculum of management courses (eg the MBA), instead of marketing, general accounts, production, etc as subjects, there would only be strategy 1, strategy 2, complements to strategy, advanced topics of strategy, more (seminars) on strategy, strategy of internationalization, etc. Obviously this does not happen for the simple reason that both strategy and the functional areas (tactics – the how) are important.[4] It should be added that in day-to-day life both strategic or tactical decisions of great or little importance can occur – see Table 2.3.[5]

Table 2.3 The importance of decisions

	Very Important	Not Very Important	Long-term	Short-term
Strategy	Entry into a new industry	Quitting a segment and entry into a similar one in the same industry	Entry into a new geographical area	Quitting one segment
Tactics	Substitution of advertising on TV by radio or newspaper	Change of publicity from programme X to Y on CNN	Construction of a new factory	Merchandising campaign

The idea in some literature that strategy refers to the long-term and tactics to the short-term is neither useful nor correct. It is not useful because it is never clear how to differentiate between short- and long-term. Where does 'long-term' begin? After a year? Eighteen months? Two years? The idea is not correct; strategic decisions can be short-term (to be implemented immediately) or acted upon later, as shown in Table 2.3. Similarly, tactical decisions can last for a long or short time.

Thus the concept of strategy used as a synonym for *where* and the concept of tactics as a synonym for *how* makes more sense, is simpler and more useful. However, it is not surprising that certain confusion exists in management literature regarding the meaning of the word 'strategy', as strategy is the most recently developed area of knowledge within management (end of the 1970s and beginning of the 1980s).[6] Other areas, such as accounting, production and finance, started and developed earlier (see Figure 2.2).[7]

APPLYING THE CONCEPT OF STRATEGY TO BUSINESS

How can these concepts from military art be transferred to business? Which decisions correspond to strategy and which correspond to tactics? As tactics refer to the functional departments, there are three types of strategic decisions in business, as shown in Figures 2.3 and 2.4.

1   In which geographical areas will the business venture to operate (attempt to invoice, attract clients): Mexico? Catalonia? United States? Canada? Belgium? etc.

Area of business administration \ Development date	End of the 19th century	Start of the 20th century	End of the1930s	End of the1950s	Start of the1960s	End of the1960s	Start of the1970s	End of the 70s and start of the 80s
Administrative	✓							
Accounting	✓							
Production Management		✓						
Human Resources			✓					
Finance				✓				
General Management					✓			
Management Information System						✓		
Marketing							✓	
Strategy								✓

Figure 2.2 Development dates of knowledge in management

2   In which industry(ies) in each geographical area will the business venture to operate: Textiles? Footwear? Hotels? Crystal? Wine? Paper pulp? Distribution? etc.

3   In which segment(s) in each industry and each geographical area will the business venture to operate? If the chosen industry is textiles and clothing, will it go into hat making? sports clothes? Swimwear? Underclothing? Furnishing materials? T-shirts? Polo necks? Carpets, Fitted carpets and runners? Trousers and shirts?

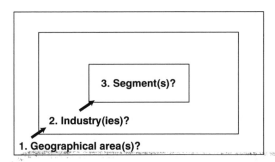

Figure 2.3 The three aspects of the strategic 'where' in management

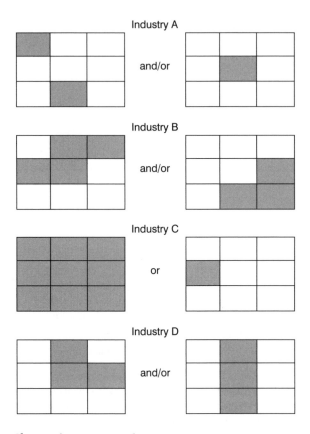

Figure 2.4 Choice of segments and areas

As Figure 2.4 shows, the alternative strategies a company might choose to follow are innumerable (N geographical areas x Y industries x K segments), but in practice they always involve one (or more) of three kinds of decisions: choice of the geographical area; choice of industry; choice of segment.

Therefore, when Philip Morris bought Miller, then Seven Up and then sold this division to Pepsi Cola, three strategic decisions were involved. The first two are the entrance into two new industries (from tobacco into beer and soft drinks) and the last is the departure from the second new industry. Philip Morris altered the *where* in terms of industry on three occasions.

Similarly, when at a certain time in the history of General Electric it entered the computer industry and then sold its manufacturing division to Honeywell, two strategic decisions were taken, both referring to industry (but not to the geographical area nor the segment). However, when

Porsche stopped making the economic Porsche (Volks-Porsche) and when Dec launched minicomputers these were two strategic decisions but here they refer to segments of the market.[8] Finally, when Volkswagen announced some years ago that it was going to abandon the US market that was also a strategic decision, but was connected with the geographical area (see Figure 2.5).

As Figure 2.6 illustrates, examples can always be found of the three kinds of strategic decisions when looking through a newspaper or magazine referring to any industry. Examples referring to geographical areas include alliances between Banco Comercial Português (BCP) and Cariplo, Bital and the Banco Popular Español (later substituted by the Central-

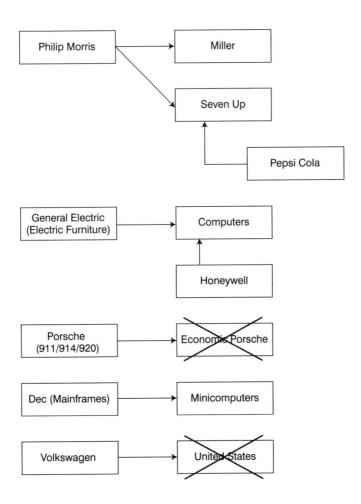

Figure 2.5 Examples of strategic moves

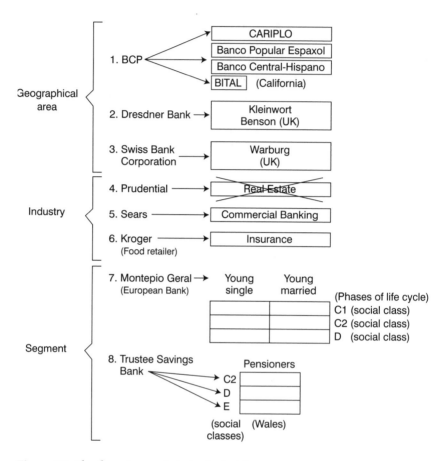

Figure 2.6 The three types of strategic decisions

Hispano) in order to use the networks of these banks' agencies to sell financial products to Portuguese emigrants in France. Similar instances are the entry of the German bank, Dresdner Bank, to trading in the United Kingdom when it acquired Kleinwort Benson; and the acquisition of another British bank, Warburg, by the Swiss Bank Corporation (SBC).

Figure 2.6 also provides examples of strategic moves in the financial area: concentration in their original *industry* as a result of Prudential leaving real estate; the entry of both Sears and Kroger to the market. The last two examples in Figure 2.6 refer to *segments*.

The case of the Trustee Savings Bank illustrates the flexibility of strategic moves within these segments. This bank decided to concentrate on one geographical area only: Wales. Within this area it concentrated on retail banking and not on corporate banking. Finally, within the retail banking it focused on the segment consisting of retired people in classes

Social class / Phase of life cycle	Young single (YS)	Young married (YM)	First home (FH)	Full home	Empty home (EH)	Old single (OS)	Pension-ers (P)	Survivors (S)
A								
B								
C1								
C2								
D							WALES	
E								

Note: Young single – not married
Young married – married and no children
First home – first child is below four years old
Full home – oldest child is above four years old
Empty home – when first child leaves home
Old single – divorcees or people who have never married
Pensioners – one or both people are retired
Survivors – only one of the pensioners lives on

Figure 2.7 Trustee Savings Bank strategy

C2, D and E. The Trustee Savings Bank has almost 90 per cent of its invoicing there (see Figure 2.7).[9]

TEN IMPORTANT ASPECTS OF STRATEGY

At this point, it is important to note ten particular aspects of the concept of strategy in business. First of all, in a company, what is the objective that underlies the definition of strategy? Very simply it is the maximization of profit. William McGowan of MCI was asked what MCI stood for; he said, 'Money Coming In'. Everything else – choice of segments, industries, geographical options – contributes to this objective.[10]

Second, what are the basic criteria according to which strategy is defined? There are two main types of criteria. One is attractiveness (margin of profit, size and foreseeable growth rate). The other is competitive advantage in its two aspects: synergy between segments (the same or different industries and geographical areas) and the degree to which

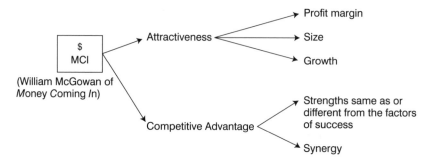

Figure 2.8 Criteria defining strategy

the strong points are the same or different from the critical factors of success (see Figure 2.8).

Third, what is the relationship between this concept of strategy and the typologies of strategy presented in the literature, such as: maintenance, concentration, extension, geographical diversification, related diversification (further subdivided into technological and market) and unrelated diversification? The usefulness of the military concept of strategy is illustrated by the simplicity of the relationship of this concept to these typologies. 'Maintenance' refers to the decision of a company to remain in the *same* segments, industries and geographical areas. The strategy will be the same in the future as in the past. 'Concentration' refers to the decision of a company to remain in *fewer* segments and/or industries and/or geographical areas. 'Extension' refers to the situation in which a company enters into *more* segments of the same industry. 'Diversification' can refer to the industry or geographical area. In the former it can be for similar or different industries. If they are similar they can be alike in technological or market terms.

What some literature defines as strategies of increase or reduction of the market quota is connected with a later phase in strategic planning, ie with the establishment of concrete objects and time limits for the company's business units which are dedicated to the various segments. The establishment of objectives is another matter involving market quota, anticipated profit, etc.[11]

A fourth aspect is linked with the *strategy analysis unit*, which in the case of *demand* is the *market segment* and in the case of *supply* is the *strategic group*. Market segment has implications in terms of what the tactics should be (organization and operation of the functional departments). The strategic group allows certain conclusions to be drawn regarding industry. Each one of these aspects will be looked at briefly.

A segment is a sub-group of clients with like needs but distinct from

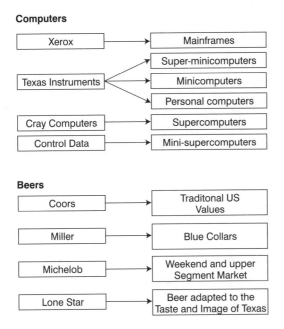

Figure 2.9 More examples of strategic moves

other sub-groups of clients. They give importance to one aspect (eg price) when acquiring a product, while other sub-groups of clients are more concerned about such things as durability, rapid delivery, design, comfort or size. A critical factor of success is the importance given to an aspect by a segment of clients. Thus the critical factors of success vary from segment to segment within an industry. The market segment is the analysis unit, the strategic decision cell.

In the beer-brewing industry, Lone Star adapted its taste and packaging to the preferences of the population of Texas. Michelob aimed at the upper segments of the market,[12] Miller went for the blue collars, Coors for the admirers of the life style and traditional image of the Midwest.[13]

In the computer industry, Cray Computers specializes in supercomputers. It examined the possibility of manufacturing mini-supercomputers but opted not to do so. The supercomputers segment was abandoned by Control Data some years ago. At the present time Texas Instruments makes personal computers and stopped manufacturing minis and super-minicomputers, Xerox started making mainframes, and so on (see Figure 2.9).

In fifth place, it is important to note that the tactics to follow (ie the organization and operation of the functional departments) depend on and

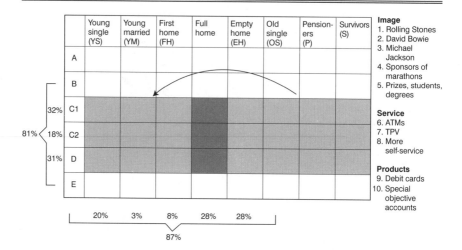

Figure 2.10 Strategy adopted by the Montepio Geral Bank

vary with the chosen strategy. The strategy determines the tactics. The option for one or another segment (industry/geographical area) has implications for the functional departments. Let us look at some examples.

Figure 2.10 illustrates the case of a European bank, the Montepio Geral, which started a strategic movement in 1991 to attract younger clients (from the same social classes as previously: C1, C2 and D). As a result of this strategic movement which began in 1991, the Montepio Geral had 87 per cent of its invoicing in the first five phases of the life cycle in 1993 (and 81 per cent in the above-mentioned social classes). To attract the younger type of client, the Montepio Geral developed a series of new marketing activities (eg sponsorship of concerts given by the Rolling Stones, David Bowie and Michael Jackson, as well as several marathons and awarded prizes to the best students of management degrees in various universities). New products were launched, such as debit cards and accounts for specific purposes (eg student accounts, accounts for the acquisition of cars). The service level speculated more on the automated teller machines (ATMs), sales terminals and on giving autonomy to the branches. That is, the venture into new segments (alteration of strategy) implied alterations in marketing and production (ie in the functional/tactical departments).

It should noted that the tactical level of alterations occurred in spite of the fact that the alteration in strategy was not very profound as:

1   The geographical area is the *same*;

2   The industry *remained the same*;

1 Subcompacts	2 Compacts	3 Overcompacts	4 Station wagons	5 Vans Light trucks
6 Trucks	7 Sports cars +70	8 Sports cars up to 70	9 Buses +70	10 Luxury +70
11 Luxury 40 – 70	12 Motorbikes up to 125	13 Motorbikes 175 – 750	14 Motorbikes +750	15 Urban ladies 2nd Car
16 Luxury – 40	17 Four-wheel drive Low Price	18 Four-wheel drive High Quality	19 Safety	20 Special vehicles (armoured, passengers, transport, etc)

Figure 2.11 Matrix of the segmentation of the car industry

3 The previous segments *were not abandoned* (new ones were added);

4 The new segments were *similar* to the previous segments as the size of the segmentation matrix – the social class – remained constant.

Another example of the impact of strategic alterations in tactics, even when the alterations are small, can be found in the car industry. Figure 2.11 shows a possible matrix of industry segmentation. BMW, which initially focused on the luxury segment of less than US $40,000, later also entered the luxury segment of US $40–70,000.

Although BMW were dealing with two of the most similar segments in the industry, various modifications had to be made in the tactics (ie operation of the functional departments). For example, let us look at three modifications in marketing which took place in the areas of sales promotion, public relations and publicity.

In sales promotion terms, the New York showrooms moved to one of the best sites in Park Avenue, to try to capitalize on the prestige of the area, for the sake of the prestige of the product. With reference to public relations, in addition to the already existing tennis and squash tournaments, sponsorship of polo and skiing was initiated, as these activities were patronized by the new clients BMW wanted to attract.[14]. In terms of publicity, the slogans in the luxury segment of less than US $40,000 emphasized: durability, credibility and value for money (including the second-hand market). Now, for the cars in the US $40–70,000 segment, the publicity slogans were altered to emphasize security, sophistication and luxury.

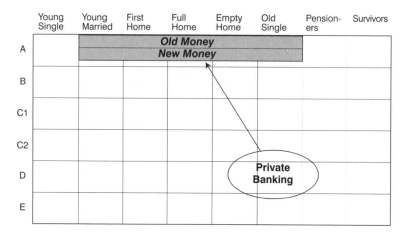

Figure 2.12 Private banking

It should be noted (in sixth place in the list of strategies) that strategy always has an impact on tactics, regardless of however small the modification of the former might be. The above examples illustrate tactical modifications even when the new segments (strategic alterations) are similar to the old. Tactical changes are also needed when the segment remains the same but the *niche* (area within *different* segments) is altered. Figure 2.12 represents private banking within the retail bank. Within private banking two niches can be seen: the so-called old money (traditionally rich people) and new money (*nouveaux riches*). Although both niches share a passion for sophisticated financial products (common in the private banking segment) they also differ from one another: the old money favours saving time and therefore the instruments allowing it, while the new money favours aspects conferring status and prestige. The *nouveaux riches* enjoy luxurious decoration, publicity-invoking prestigious figures who were clients in the past – such as Oliver Cromwell and the Adams & Co Bank, golden and platinum-coloured cheques, etc (see Figure 2.13).[15,16]

A seventh aspect of strategy worth noting is that the segment must be precisely defined. To do that four elements must be indicated:

1 The product;

2 The geographical area;

3 The need;

4 The client.

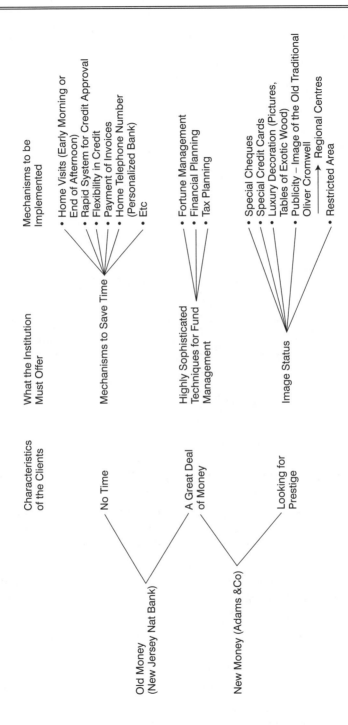

Figure 2.13 Financial products

A B E		E		E	
	A		A B		
C D	B E			A B	
		C D			
		C D	C	C	

Figure 2.14 Examples of strategic groups in an industry

The product itself defines the industry (financial services and cars, footwear, etc). By adding the geographical area the location of the industry is defined, which is important as at times adaptations have to be made to local tastes.[17] By defining the need, an indication is given of the critical factors of success characterizing the segment (luxury, comfort, durability). By indicating the clients, the sub-group of clientele is revealed to which the product is directed. A segment of the market is a sub-group of *clients* with specific *needs*, buying a *product* in a certain *geographical area*. When defining a segment of the market these four elements must be indicated.[18]

In eighth place, if in strategy the analysis unit on the side of demand (clients) is the market segment, on the side of supply (companies) the analysis unit is the *strategic group*. The strategic group is an important concept from which various assumptions can be made about an industry. Figure 2.14 shows a hypothetical industry with 30 segments and five companies in it (A, B, C, D and E) and the strategic positions of the various companies in the industry. Some segments are empty (for the time being companies do not take up a position for reasons of attractiveness or other factors). A strategic group is a group of companies which occupy approximately the same segments, that is, they follow very similar strategies. Companies A and B share three of the five segments in which they operate. Companies C and D also share three of five segments but as there are no segments in which company D is and in which C is not present, C and D form a more similar strategic group than A nd B. Company E is a group on its own, as there is no other company with a similar strategy.

The concept of strategic group is important because, when an industry is taken and the strategic groups existing in it are defined, very interesting conclusions can be reached about the industry; for example, with reference to synergy and possible future strategic moves of the companies belonging to it. Synergy between the segments it is much *greater* when both the number of groups is *lower* than the number of companies in the industry[19] and the number of segments common to all the companies of the strategic groups is greater than the number of segments in which only some of the companies of the various strategic groups are present.

By looking at the strategic groups in an industry it is also possible to foresee the future strategic movements of its companies. For example, it is very natural that as soon as company D has resources to enter other segments, it will enter the segments where company C is alone at the moment, as they should be the most synergetic.[20]

A ninth important aspect of strategy is the clarification between strategic option (decision) and global service. Nowadays in many industries (auditing, environment, electronic equipment, packaging, banking, etc), there is a tendency to offer global service; that is, to define the service in terms of need, not product (see Figure 2.15 and Figure 2.16).[21] This is *to avoid losing a client* to a competitor for not offering a certain product that could be supplied by the competitor and to provide the client with *greater satisfaction and loyalty* by saving time. This is different from the strategic decision concerning the option to favour certain types of clients to the detriment of others. In other words, one possibility is to opt for a certain type of client (market segment); another is, having opted to cater for a certain type of client, to give them everything related to a certain need in order to satisfy them, keep their loyalty and provide a high degree of satisfaction.

Finally, a tenth and last aspect. In strategy there are two things which are distinct: present strategy and future strategy. Present strategy is not a matter of subjective opinion but a question of objective fact. In order to know the present strategy of a company it is not necessary to ask anyone anything – but just look where it invoices (in which segments, industries and geographical areas). The determination of the present strategy is simply a matter of the list of clients.[22]

Whether that is the desired strategy or not is another question. That is the reason for making a strategic plan – to evaluate the present strategy and see if it should be kept or if there is another one which is better, to define the future strategy.

Therefore a strategic plan is a document like any other (organizational chart, financial budget), which must be made according to certain rules. A financial budget indicates: income, outgoing cash and its source, while

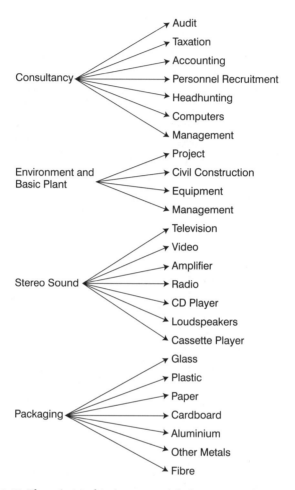

Figure 2.15 The relationship between global service and strategic decisions

a specific organizational chart shows the hierarchical and functional relationships within the company. Similarly, a strategic plan is a simple document which must indicate three things: the *geographical areas* in which it is going to venture; within these geographical areas, the *industries* in which it will advance; and within these industries, the *segments* which it will back. How to prepare a strategic plan is the theme of the next chapter.

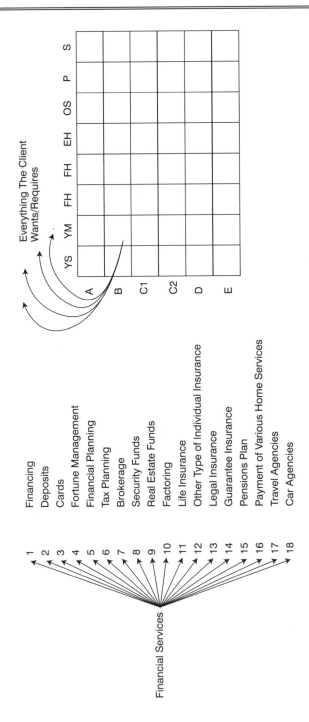

Figure 2.16 Financial services: global services and strategic decisions

3

How to prepare a strategic plan

Peter F Drucker (photograph by courtesy of Executive Digest)

INTRODUCTION

As the previous chapter indicated, there are two main types of strategy: for the present, and for the future. Current strategy is not a matter of subjective opinion, but a question of objective fact. In order to know the current strategy of a company it is not necessary to ask anyone anything – but just to see where it is operating (in which segments, industries and geographical areas). To ascertain the current strategy of any institution is simply a matter of obtaining a list of clients, of knowing where the firm presently invoices.

Whether the present strategy is the most desirable strategy or not is another question. That is the reason for making a strategic plan: to assess the current strategy and to see if it should be retained. If a better strategy exists, then the present one will need redefinition. A strategic plan is a document like any other (eg organization chart, financial budget). It must be drawn up according to certain rules. How to prepare a strategic plan is the subject of this chapter. In addition, several examples are given in here of what a strategic plan looks like.

The criteria involved in preparing a strategic plan are: *attractiveness* (sales volume, rate of growth, profit margin); *competitive position* (strengths and key success factors); and *synergy*. A strategic plan must have three main characteristics: *synthesis, simplicity* and *incisiveness*. Let's see how to attain this.

> *Simplicity makes for clarity. Complexity creates problems of communication.*
>
> PETER F DRUCKER, MANAGEMENT, TASKS, PRINCIPLES AND RESPONSIBILITIES

DESCRIPTION OF A STRATEGIC PLAN

A strategic plan is an extremely simple document. It should always be *simple* and *condensed*. It will consist of four or a maximum of five pages for most companies. For larger groups it will have at the most about 12 pages. Let us have a look at its visual aspect.

The *first page* (see Figure 3.1) of the plan must refer to the geographical area in which the company operates and to the company's strategy in

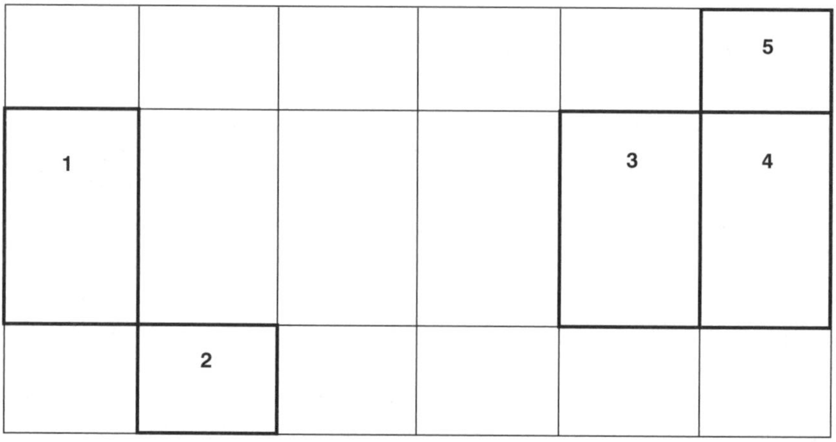

Figure 3.1 The first page of the strategic plan

that geographical area. To save paper at the top of this page, the segmentation matrix of the industry in which the company operates in this geographical area should be shown; that is, the group of segments in that industry. Then the segmentation matrix will be used to indicate the segments in which the company *is* and *is not operating* (segments 1–5 in Figure 3.1).

The segmentation matrix of the industry must show:

1   All the segments of the *industry*;

2   All the segments in which the company *is*;

3   All the segments in which the company *is not*.

These are the rules to follow.

The *following pages* of the strategic plan are to justify the venture into the above segments. Therefore these pages refer to the segments in which the organization is, and are as many as the number of those segments. A page is assigned to each segment the choice of which has been justified. This justification is based on three criteria: *attractiveness, competitive position* and *synergy*. Figure 3.2 indicates the elements which should be included on each page and Figure 3.3 provides a hypothetical example.

As can be seen in Figures 3.2 and 3.3, on the top of each page dedicated to a segment, the name of this segment of the market must be indicated. In order to be correctly described it must contain *four* elements: the *product*; the *need* satisfied; the type of *client* targeted and the *geographical area* of activity. An example for a footwear company would be the segment of: shoes (product) for women (client) in the United States (geographical area), with emphasis on comfort (need). This is the segment of Mabel, Campor, Scholl Manufacturing Co, etc. Other examples: boots in PVC for seamen in Galicia, ensuring waterproofing (segment of the make Edmar); boots for postmen and soldiers in all Europe with great resistance and durability (segment of Sindocal); cork-soled wooden shoes for nurses in clinics and hospitals in the north of the country ensuring silence, and so on.

ATTRACTIVENESS

Once the segment has been defined, the first criterion to need justification is *attractiveness*. This is the amount of profit available in this segment of the market, and which the company will try to collect within a period of three to five years.

Definition of the Segment

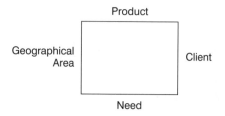

Attractiveness

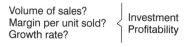

Competitive Position

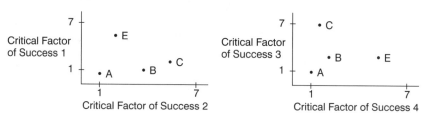

Note: E=Our company; A,B,C=three main competitors

$$\text{Competitive Position} = \frac{\text{Average E} - \text{Average (A,B and C)}}{\text{Average (A,B and C)}} \times 100$$

Synergy

$$\text{Synergy} = \frac{\text{Costs Saved}}{\text{Total Cost}} \times 100$$

Figure 3.2 Elements of a strategic plan

Segment

Large air compressors
of more than 1 000 steam
horsepower, produced in
small series in United States
for units of the manufacturing
industry

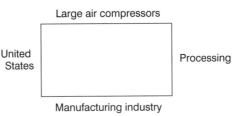

United
States

Large air compressors

Processing

Manufacturing industry

Attractiveness

Sales volume   = US$ 200 million ⎫ Average ROI next
Margin per unit sold= US$ 18/20 million ⎬ 3 years = 18%
Growth rate   = 2–3%   ⎭

Competitive Position[1]

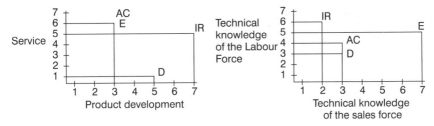

Note: E=Our company; IR=Ingersoll Rand; D=Dresser; AC=Allis Chalmers
(Three main competitors)

$$\text{Competitive Position} = \frac{\text{Average E (5) } - \text{ Average of (AC; IR; D)(4)}}{\text{Average of (AC; IR; D)(4)}} \times 100 = 25\%$$

Synergy

$$\frac{\underset{\text{Suppliers}}{10\% \text{ discount}} + \underset{\text{Sales force}}{\text{Sharing of } \frac{1}{2}} + \underset{\text{Service team}}{\text{Sharing of } \frac{1}{2}} + \underset{\text{in warehouse}}{\text{Saving of } 25\%} + \underset{\text{on machinery}}{\text{Saving of } 15\%}}{\text{Budget of the total cost of company specialized in the segment}} \times 100 = 12\%$$

[1] The amounts attributed to Allis Chalmers, Dresser and Ingersoll Rand are merely hypothetical
and are not any assessment of value.

Figure 3.3   Example of a strategic plan

	Average Annual	Average Cumulative Value for the Period
Profit in Absolute Terms	1	3
ROI	2	4

Note: 1, 2, 3, and 4 =Options to combine the three subvariables in the 3–5 year period.

Figure 3.4 Four ways of combining the three subvariables of attractiveness

It is useful to distinguish three aspects of attractiveness:

1   *Volume* of foreseeable sales of the segment;

2   The *margin* it is hoped to achieve for unit of the product sold;

3   The *growth rate* over the next three to five years.

Of course, the higher these values the more attractive the segment will be. In practice, some segments will be more attractive than others. Therefore it is useful to combine the three subvariables of attractiveness under just one value. That can be done by using the variable profit (in absolute value) or profitability (in return on investment [ROI] terms – investment profitability[1]). In any case, either the cumulative value for a period of three to five years or the average annual value for this period can be used (see Figure 3.4).[2] The four options are schematized in Figure 3.4; if they are not exactly equivalent they still produce similar results in practical terms.

The need to summarize all three attractiveness variables in a single index (1, 2, 3 or 4 in Figure 3.4) comes from the fact that these variables are not perfectly correlated. So, one segment can rate higher in one variable and lower in another, or vice versa. However, in general terms there is some relationship between the variables which can be summarized as in Table 3.1.

The reasons are:

1   Higher rates of growth are usually found in the early phases of the product life cycle, when sales volume is lower. Therefore, a negative relation occurs in cells 2 and 4;

Table 3.1 Correlations of attractiveness variables

Correlation between variables within *any* segment X	Sales volume		Rate of growth		Profit margin	
Sales volume	1)	1	4)	-	7)	-
Rate of growth	2)	-	5)	1	8)	+
Profit margin	3)	-	6)	+	9)	1

2   Mature markets (lower rates of growth) tend to be more competitive. Therefore, in general, there is a positive relation between growth rate and profit margin (less competition) in cells 6 and 8; and

3   There is a negative relation between sales volume (mature markets) and profit margins (cells 3 and 7).

Relations 1, 2 and 3 are to be found in general. However, in each concrete situation, the concrete value of the correlation will vary.

THE COMPETITIVE POSITION OF THE COMPANY

The second aspect to be indicated on the page dedicated to each segment in the strategic plan is the estimate of what the competitive position of the company might be in that segment. The attractiveness (or profitability) of the segment is important but it is an average estimate for the segment. For example, it might be estimated that a segment would grow on average between 5 per cent and 7 per cent in the next three to five years. Some companies will grow more and others less. Some companies will be above the average, others lower. That is why the average is a dangerous statistic. For example, if a person has his head in a refrigerator and his feet in an oven, his 'average' temperature is reasonable, but he certainly will not feel very well.[3]

The question is: Will our company be *above* or *below* the average values of attractiveness indicated for the segment? That depends on the competitive position of our company in that market segment. If it has competitive superiority it will be above the average, if it has competitive inferiority it will be below the average.

The competitive position of a company is the consequence of the qualities or defects it possesses in what is important. In the literature, the qualities of companies are designated *strong points*, the defects as *weak points*; and what are important are the *critical factors of success*.

Let us start with these. In any segment of the market a company must do dozens of tasks satisfactorily to serve the client. It has to offer good service, a good image and suitable distribution channels; it has to have minimally sophisticated equipment, in technological terms; it must have trained, motivated and satisfied factory workers (with low absenteeism and rotation); the location of its factories must be appropriate; the product development department must be of good quality; the sales force must have good technical and marketing knowledge, etc. All of this is important.

However, empirical evidence shows that, in order to attain a good performance, there are particular tasks which are more important than others for each market segment. There are three methods for finding the critical factors of success which, as they are satisfactorily explained elsewhere, will not be developed in detail here. They are: analysis of the risk (of operation and delivery); analysis of the client; and path analysis. To paraphrase George Orwell, all the variable tasks are equally important for good performance, but some are more important than others.

For example, in large air compressors of more than 1,000 horsepower made in small series, the most important variables are: service; the technical knowledge possessed by the workforce; the technical knowledge of the sales force; and the development and applied research department (see Figure 3.3).[4] The *service* offered by the manufacturer (quality and speed) is a critical factor of success because the opportunity cost of the possibility of bad or non-functioning of a compressor of this kind is high. In certain cases, entire sections of the factory have to stop. The *technical knowledge of the workforce* is vital as each compressor is unique (they are made one by one or in small series). Here – in contrast with a production-line where the worker is still and the product moves – the compressor is still and the teams of workers go around it. Each week the work on the compressors is at least slightly different.

The *technical knowledge of the sales force* is also a critical factor of success, as the sale of a product of this kind is based on plans and detailed engineering proposals, analysed by the purchaser's technical representative. That is why most of the salespersons of manufacturers of this type of compressor are engineers. The *development and applied research department* is also critical as each compressor is made to measure, in accordance with the client's specifications.

These variables, which are extremely important for the good performance in a certain sector of the market, are called critical factors of success. In each market segment[5] there are a maximum of five critical factors of success.[6]

It is important to note that the critical factors of success are something belonging to an activity, whether it be business or sport or something else. For example, one of the critical factors of success in basketball is height; for a jockey it is weight (lack of); for a Japanese sumo wrestler it is also weight (but now its presence); in chess it is memory and deductive logic. In contrast, strong points (qualities) and weaknesses (faults) do not apply to an activity but an entity (person, company or country). In practice, no entity has only strong points or only weak points but a mixture of both. For example, some companies will give better service than their competitors, but will achieve limited penetration in the distribution channels; others may have a better image but be less competitive in terms of price, and so on. Therefore in Figure 3.3, no company (in the second graph) is top in everything. If that should happen, the company would be in the northeast corner of the graph.

The *competitive position* of a company is determined by whether it has strong points (qualities) or weaknesses (faults) in the critical factors of success (the three or four most important variables in each market segment). What is its *mark* (eg on a scale of one to seven) in the key variables for success? Whether these marks are *above* or *below* the average of the companies in the segment referring to the variables of attractiveness (growth rate, margin and sales quota) will determine its relative position.

It is possible to visualize the competitive position of a company using Cartesian graphs (see Figures 3.2 and 3.3), the axes of which show marks for different critical factors of success The specific position occupied by the company (from one to seven) depends on how its strong and weak points compare with those of the competition. Figure 3.2 presents the elements which must appear in general terms and Figure 3.3 represents a hypothetical example.

The three best competitors (those having a larger quota of the market) in a certain segment are usually used as standard for comparison. For example, in Figure 3.3, our imaginary company (E) has a quality of service equal to Ingersoll Rand (IR) and the product development department has a level equal to Allis Chalmers (AC). Allis Chalmers has the best service; Ingersoll Rand has the best product development department. The technical knowledge of our sales force is superior to that of all our competitors, as are the qualifications of the workers with the exception of Ingersoll Rand.

The use of Cartesian graphs allows the competitive position of the company to be visualized and compared with the competitors in a certain segment of the market. In addition, it is possible very simply to summarize this competitive position in one value. Thus we can tell whether our company is 25, 10 or 5 per cent below or above the average of our three best competitors.

To do this, proceed as follows. First, calculate the average marks of our company in each of the critical factors of success. For example, in the segment in Figure 3.3 our company's average is $(5+3+5+7)/4 = 5$. Then, do the same for each of the three main competitors. Thus, the average of competitor AC in the four critical factors of success is $(6+3+4+3)/4 = 4$; Dresser's average is $(1+5+3+3)/4=3$; IR's average is $(5+7+6+2)/4 = 5$.[7]

Third, the average of the three main competitors is calculated which, in this case, is $(4+3+5)/3=4$. Finally, to summarize the competitive position of our company in face of the competition, calculate the relative percentage below or above the competitors (in terms of its value in the critical factors of success): $(5-4)/4 = 25$ per cent above. In the specific example in Figure 3.3, our competitive position is approximately 25 per cent higher than the competitors and not 30 per cent more, 20 per cent more, 10 per cent more, 5 per cent less or 15 per cent less which would be possible values in other situations.

This number (which is a simplification as it just focuses on the three main competitors) is a valuable synthesis in that it expresses in a simple percentage value how our company is placed versus its main competitors in terms of strong and weak points in the critical factors of success.[8] This is written into the strategic plan, so that when it is being re-evaluated a year later there is a simultaneously *clear* and *detailed* awareness of what influenced us to venture into this segment. At the same time, it is possible to see whether the previous evaluation (and resulting venture in the segment) is to be maintained or not.[9, 10]

SYNERGY

The third criterion which can persuade a company to be present in a certain segment, and must be included on the corresponding page for each segment in a strategic plan, is *synergy*. Synergy comes from the Greek word *synergos* meaning the cumulative effect of various strengths. In the same way as the competitive position of a company in a segment can be summarized in a percentage so too synergy is, in its essence, a number. This number refers to the *sharing* between two or more segments.[11]

The question is: How does a company *allocate* its sales force, distribution fleet, warehousing, suppliers, etc between two market segments that it occupies? No such decision would be needed if the company dealt as two distinct autonomous companies, each one working in a different segment. But that would require *duplication* of all the resources and therefore the costs. Costs might be lower if autonomous companies combined to form two divisions of a whole – a larger company. *The lower these costs, the greater is the value of the synergy.*

Once the concept is clear, the calculation of synergy can be made in an extremely simple way by means of a *ratio*. Everything *spent* is placed in the *denominator* if the division working in a certain segment of the market is an autonomous company. The expenditure is the list of all the necessary resources to operate in a given segment of the market and which are part of the business plan, including the number of workers to be hired, the number and type of machines necessary, the test laboratory to be established, the number of salespeople needed, etc (see Figures 3.2 and 3.3). All this is evaluated in money.

What is *saved* (by dealing as divisions of a larger company instead of acting as two autonomous companies) is put in the *numerator*. If more than 10 per cent discount is obtained on quantity of raw materials X or on components Y because the suppliers sell a greater volume as they invoice two divisions and not just one, the savings this represents are recorded. If the sales force of the other division is used, only 50 per cent of the salespeople will be needed than would otherwise be necessary. This saving is also recorded, and so on. The same occurs for other economized resources: a hypothesis is that the service team costs 50 per cent, storage costs 25 per cent and the use of machines 15 per cent (see Figure 3.2). The ratio containing the cost savings in the numerator and the total costs (which would be incurred if the company were autonomous) in the denominator gives the synergy. This value can be 25 per cent plus, 15 per cent plus, 5 per cent plus, etc. [12] In the specific example in Figure 3.2, the value of synergy is 12 per cent.[13]

Briefly, the reason for the choice of a segment can be summarized in three numbers:

- Profitability (eg 18 per cent);
- Competitive position (+ 25 per cent);
- Synergy (+12 per cent) (see example in Figure 3.2).

These three numbers, which should appear on the page of the strategic plan referring to each segment of the market, act as a reminder – months after the plan has been made or when it is consulted or revised – of the reasons which at a certain moment influenced the venture into a certain segment of the market.

Any other information, over and above these three numbers, is *unnecessary*. Unnecessary details have two drawbacks: they need *time* to be written and therefore represent *costs* without practical consequences; and they *obscure* what is essential. In other words, they are a waste of time and an exercise in folly. Figures 3.5 and 3.6 provide other examples of strategic plans, for the electronic security equipment and floor treatment industries.

ABROAD

The scheme to be followed in the preparation of the strategic plan is the same if the company should decide to venture into markets outside its home territory. First, the geographical area is indicated: Catalonia, Mexico, Benelux countries, Canada, etc. Then the segmentation matrix of the industry in which it is desired to venture for each geographical area is presented. That industry can be the same or different from the industry of the company in its home territory, say the US. Then, although the industry might be the same the segments making up all the industry *can be* different from those existing in the United States (due to the differences between the markets). Finally the segments in which it has been decided to venture can be the same as those in the United States *or* other countries. For these three reasons for each foreign country or region a segmentation matrix should be presented.[14]

In any case each segment must be justified in the same way as is done for all the segments on the national market: a page per segment, with three criteria: attractiveness, competitive position and synergy. Briefly, the presentation analysis and scheme prepared for the national market must be repeated for each foreign area, neither more nor less. A summary is

Definition of the Segment

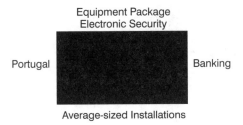

Portugal — Equipment Package Electronic Security — Banking

Average-sized Installations

Attractiveness

Sales Volume (thousands escudos)   0.5 Million
Margin per Unit sold   15%   → Average ROI next 3 years   15%
Growth Rate   5%

Competitive Position[1]

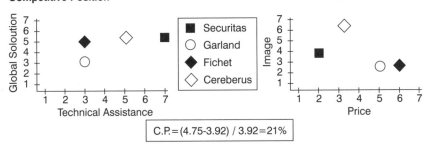

C.P. = (4.75-3.92) / 3.92 = 21%

Synergy

$$S = 30\% = 100 \times \frac{\text{Sales Force 50\% + Spec. Tech. 40\% + Supp. 15\% + Warehouse 10\%}}{\text{Budget of Company Specialized in the Segment}}$$

[1] Note: The ratings attributed to the firms are merely hypothetical and do not constitute any real assessment of value.

Figure 3.5 Strategic plan for a target segment in electronic security equipment

Segment: Treatment of Pavements

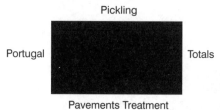

Pickling

Portugal   Totals

Pavements Treatment

Attractiveness

Sales Volume	Growth Rate	Gross Margin	Average ROI next three years
2 200 000 thousand escudos	2% per year	49%	18.5%

Competitive Position=50% [1]

Complete line of
Products + Machinery + Accessories

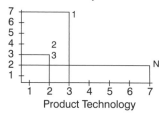

Product Technology

Technical Knowledge of the
Sales Force

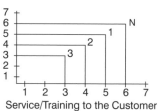

Service/Training to the Customer

Note: 1 – Lever-Taski; 2 – Henkel; 3 – Triquimica; N – Us

Synergy 24.7%

Nature of Cost	Sales Force	Transport	Warehouse	Technical Services	Fixed Cost	Total
Real	98 000	17 000	15 000	0	55 000	185 000
Forecast	35 000	18 000	20 000	0	70 000	143 000
Synergy	29.0%	6.0%	26.0%	0.0%	21%	22.7%

[1]Note: the ratings attributed to the firms are merely hypothetical and do not
        constitute any real assessment of value.

Figure 3.6 Strategic plan for a target segment in the floor industry

given in Figure 3.7 which presents several first pages of the geographical sections of a strategic plan of a hypothetical company in the footwear industry in the United States and Catalonia and in garment manufacturing in Germany.

PRINCIPLES TO BE FOLLOWED IN A STRATEGIC PLAN

In conclusion, it is possible briefly to list the characteristics which a strategic plan must observe. They are three: synthesis, simplicity and clarity.

Synthesis

This principle can be called *Oscar Wilde's motto*. At the end of a letter to a friend, he wrote: 'I apologize for the length of this letter but I did not have enough time to make it shorter.'[15] Synthesis is the first characteristic of any strategic plan. It only needs and therefore should only have N + 1 pages, where N is the number of segments in which the company is present, and 1 the first page where the segmentation matrix of the industry is immediately presented.[16]

In this segmentation matrix the following must be clearly described:

- *all* the segments of the industry;
- all those in which it *will venture*;
- those in which it will *not* venture.

Each page devoted to a segment must contain only: the *description of the segment* in exact terms (product, client, need and geographical area); and *three numbers* justifying the venture into the segment: attractiveness (profitability of the estimated capital), competitive position (percentage) and synergy (percentage of costs saved).

Anything else is simply a waste of time. Therefore when you read a document entitled 'strategic plan' but by the third paragraph (at the latest) of the first page no clear idea has been given of where the company is and is not, this document is not a strategic plan but purely a waste of time. Line managers were taken away from their daily work to do something long and vague but not to produce a pragmatic, useful working document. This is a test any plan should pass, which we will call the *third paragraph test*.[17]

Section I: Portugal

Footwear Industry				
Children	Ladies Italian fashion	Comfort	Beach (4)	Free time (2)
Men Class B	Ladies French fashion	Cold climates	Nursing	Postmen/ Army
Men Class C1 and C2	Ladies　· other fashion/design	Adherence (3)	Dancers	Sport
Men Low Price	Ladies Low price	Waterproof (1)	Orthopaedic	Others (5)

Section II: Catalonia

Footwear Industry				
Children	Ladies Italian fashion	Comfort	Beach (4)	Free time (2)
Men Class B	Ladies French fashion	Cold climates	Nursing	Postmen/ Army
Men Class C1 and C2	Ladies other fashion/design	Adherence (3)	Dancers	Sport
Men Low Price	Ladies Low price	Waterproof (1)	Orthopaedic	Others (5)

Figure 3.7 The first pages of the geographical sections of a strategic plan

Section III: Germany

Manufacturing Industry				
Type of Product \ Segment	A Low	B Medium-low	C Medium-high	D High
1 Underwear				
2 T-shirts and polonecks	▓			
3 Sports (sweatshirts, track suits, sweaters and shorts)	▓			
4 Swimsuits	▓			
5 Trousers and shirts				
6 Sweaters and various woollen products (6)				
7 Coats and similar (7)				
8 Millinery and leather goods				
9 Others: handkerchiefs, ties and shawls (8)				
10 Lace, embroidery and trimmings				
11 Carpets, fitted and runners				
12 Bags				
13 Waterproof canvas tarpaulins, sailcloths, nets, ropes and cables				

(1) Used by seamen, fishmen, etc, boots and PVC (eg the trade mark Edmar)
(2) Textile shoe – slippers (eg trade mark Rilago)
(3) Specially used by boatowners (eg trade mark Timberland)
(4) Including another kind of footwear specializing in coolness and lack of weight
(5) Special cases, eg large sizes, shoes providing height, etc (eg trade mark Eurico and Elevators)
(6) Jackets and scarves
(7) Overcoats, raincoats, blouses
(8) Chest, jacket, pocket

Note: The darker outline indicates the segments in which the company is present.

Simplicity (Donald Sutherland's Principle)

The famous North American actor Donald Sutherland recounted that until a certain time in his life he did not give autographs. He said that he considered it pretentious, in bad taste and he considered himself as a normal, simple person. One day he received a letter from some parents who asked him for an autograph for their son's birthday. Donald Sutherland took the time to write a three-page, polite, courteous letter, in which he apologized for not giving the requested autograph, and he explained that he considered himself as an ordinary, normal and simple person... Two weeks later he received a reply from the parents by post. Basically, it said: first, your letter is one of the most ridiculous we have ever received; second, in any case, thank you. We cut your name off the end of your letter and gave it to our son. However, *you could have simplified it from the beginning.*

Simplicity is the second characteristic which a strategic plan must have. It is not worthwhile writing many words which will do nothing but hide the essential. All that is necessary is: indication of the geographical areas; segmentation matrix of the industries in which the company does and does not operate; description of the segments in which does and does not operate; and justification (with the three basic numbers for attractiveness, competition position and synergy). Anything more is not only unnecessary but confusing, hindering perception of the essential. *More* (words) implies *less* (in understanding and comprehension). Here, as so often in life, less is more.

Phrases such as 'We intend to maximize our potential growth', or 'We seek to offer higher quality products', or 'It is our aim to obtain profit relevant to the growth of the company', or 'Our strategy is to make the assets profitable by increasing the company's profits' appear in many strategic plans. They transform these plans into Omega watches, that is they neither gain nor lose. Being tolerant I would say that 80 per cent of the strategic plans I have seen until now are veritable Omegas.[18]

Saying that a company intends to have profits is the same as saying that a person wants to be happy. That is obvious. More relevant questions are: What is that person going to do in order to be happy? What will their profession be? What sports will they practise? How will they use their free time? etc.[19] It is not necessary to say that the companies want to have profits, survive, grow, etc.[20] It is necessary to say what they are going to do (segments/industries/geographical areas) to attain that desideratum. Therefore the third principle to be followed by a strategic plan is to be clear.

Clarity

Companies must be *clear* about where the company is and is not. A strategic plan must clearly state, in terms of segments, industries and geographical areas, where it is going and not going to venture. Therefore the most important word in a strategic plan is *not*. That is why it is said that strategy is like a virtuous woman – it must know how to say no. If it is not it becomes what Michael Porter calls 'stuck in the middle'. The strategic plan is then of an undefined character and the segments into which the company will or will not venture are not known. As Alain (French poet) said, to think is to know how to say no.

A manager who prepares a grey plan, not in black and white, is like a person leaving his house with a shoe on one foot and a galosh on the other. A friend asks him, 'Why do you have a galosh?'

'It might rain.'

'Then why don't you have two galoshes?'

'It probably won't rain.'

Either it will or will not rain; similarly, the option is for some segments or others. Otherwise the person will limp all day, and companies that limp mean fewer profits.

In other words, a strategic plan without clarity, without the most important word *not*, is as if a manager were nominated Minister of Transport and decided that instead of driving on the right driving on the left would start but there would be a transitional, gradual period... The result would obviously be a disaster. Disasters in companies mean *bankruptcies*.

CONCLUSION: THE RAIN DANCE, ACCORDING TO ACKOFF

In a competitive market, success depends on an institution having either a good *strategy* or good *tactics*. *Quality of strategy* depends on an institution ameliorating the application of its resources, which are scarce (people, installations and money), and therefore they must be invested where they give better value (profit). That is, it is necessary to be selective. If we as individuals are selective in our personal life about with whom we associate and do not associate, how we use our time, where we invest our money, why should an institution not be equally selective in the

Figure 3.8 Summary of success

application of all its resources? As the popular American proverb says: 'You can do anything; you cannot do everything (at least well and at the same time).' Thus, it is important to choose the correct strategic options and then to carry them out correctly. This last aspect depends on: finding zones where our strong points correspond to the critical factors of success; occupying areas of land between which there are connections, ie, synergy; and encompassing markets with future good prospects (growth), margins and invoicing.

Quality of tactics depends not only on intrinsic aspects (a good publicity plan, merchandising, etc), but also on the suitability of the tactical plans to the strategy.

That is, as was shown in Chapter 2, a company does not have good tactics if it does not adapt its plans in the functional areas (marketing, finance, personnel, production, etc), to its strategy. Tactics can only be defined in accordance with and after deciding on strategy. For that to happen the strategy must have been well defined in formal terms.

The *formal* aspects are associated with *clear* decisions as to where resources will be used or *not* (time, money, people), thus avoiding lack of definitions whereby resources may end up being replaced by the competition. That requires the above-mentioned characteristics of synthesis, simplicity and clarity. Without them, as Russell L Ackoff mentioned (1991, *Creating the Corporate Future*, John Wiley & Sons, New York) sessions to prepare the strategic plans are transformed into rain dance meetings as they have no influence whatsoever on the rainfall (money) received by the company. This carries the nuance that at the present time some Indians (managers) have started to disbelieve in the utility of the rain dance.[21]

So the characteristics of synthesis, simplicity and clarity mean that a strategic plan is not equivalent to a mere rain dance, but has some influence on the rainfall.

The usefulness of a plan without these characteristics is zero. However, that is the good news, as the bad news is that such a plan required the managers' time (and therefore the company's money). It would have been better if the managers had not been deflected from their daily contact with clients, suppliers, managing the factory, the sales force, etc, losing time in a foolish exercise and carrying out a worthless task. Figure 3.8 summarizes this logic. The Appendix presents some examples of parts of strategic plans.[22]

4

Quantifying strategy

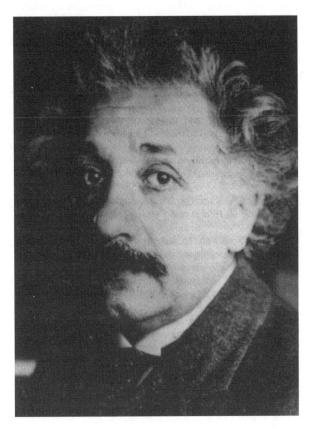

Albert Einstein

INTRODUCTION

Having described how to make a strategic plan in the previous chapter, the rest of the book will be dedicated to *measuring strategy*. The first way to measure strategy (which is the content of this chapter) is by *quantifying it*; that is, putting numbers in it, based on four variables:

- concentration;
- extension;
- competitive position;
- diversity.

The strategy of *any* firm in *any* industry can be described and defined in terms of these four variables. This chapter presents in a very simple way how to go about it and the advantages of doing so. First, by quantifying strategy it is possible to position any firm's strategy in a diagram and therefore to visualize strategy. As the Chinese proverb says, a picture is worth a thousand words.Then, by quantifying, one is able to give information in a much more precise manner than is possible using words. One says more by talking less and convergence of efforts by management follows. Finally, by quantifying a firm strategy, it is possible immediately to draw inferences about the tactics to use: as we shall see, quantification draws the attention to the paths to follow. Let us then see in very simple terms how one can quantify any firm's strategy.

> *When we give a thing a number, we know something about that thing.*
>
> ALBERT EINSTEIN

Albert Einstein said that when a thing was given a number, something was known about it. Therefore it would be interesting to quantify strategy. That is possible provided the present strategy followed by a company is a fact; as long as it is something objective which refers to its actual position on the market, where the company does and does not invoice, where it is and where it is not. If so, it can and should be evaluated.

It should be added that although strategic literature has greatly increased of late it has not been accompanied by a similar evolution in the mechanisms of measuring the concept. However, it is important to evaluate that what has been described.[1] Every company working within an industry should develop mechanisms to evaluate and characterize its performance quantitatively. For the purposes of this chapter we will assume a static, not a dynamic, point of view of the present strategy of a company in an industry and four concepts will be used: concentration, extension, competitive position and diversity (cell 2 in Figure 4.1).

There are three advantages in quantifying. First of all, by quantifying a great deal of information can be *synthesized*. For this reason it is also an important tool for evaluating strategy. Second, by coordinating the four

Concepts		Between industries	Within one industry
Viewpoint	Static	1. Relationship Vertical integration Market diversification Technological diversification	2. Concentration Extension Competitive position Diversity
	Dynamic	3. Redefinition of	4. Strategic reorientation (Chapter 7 of this book)

Figure 4.1 Aim of this chapter

variables mentioned above, two by two, in graphs, it is possible to *visualize* various kinds of strategy. Finally, *immediate implications* can be drawn from these graphs referring to the strategies the companies should follow.

THE FOUR MEASUREMENTS OF STRATEGY WITHIN AN INDUSTRY

Let us look at the segmentation matrix of a typical market, eg engineering services as presented in Figure 4.2. Cells marked with a cross represent empty segments (where no market exists)[2] and with reference to the other cells the company can invoice in them. In Figure 4.2 the amount of the invoicing of the company is registered in each cell.

A company operating in this or in any other market can follow various types of strategy: total coverage of the industry (maximizing or not, adapting to each segment of the market); partial coverage; specialization in one segment, etc. By following different strategies, companies in this market are differentiated by various dimensions.

Concentration

First of all, a company can opt for greater or lesser concentration of sales in terms of distribution among the segments that the company currently occupies (invoice).

Type of Services		Clients → A Centr. Admin.	B Reg. Admin.	C Local Admin.	D Private Industry	E Private Real-Estate	F State Owned Companies	G Cooperatives	Total
1	Special Infrastructure (Large Systems)			18%	X	X		X	18%
2	Common Infrastructure	X	X	20%	X	10%	X	X	30%
3	Water Supply Treatment								–
4	Effluent Treatment			16%					16%
5	AA. Syst Planning				X	X	X	X	–
6	Drain Syst Planning				X	X	X	X	–
7	Sewage Treat Planning				X	X	X	X	–
8	Special Sewage Works				X	X	X	X	–
9	Normal Sewage Works	X	15%		X	X	X	X	15%
10	Hydraulic Works/Dams			17%	X	X	X		17%
11	Hydraulic Works/Irrigation	1%		X	X	X	X		1%
12	Hydraulic Works/Floods			X	X	X	X		–
13	Pollution/Environment							1%	1%
14	Project management						2%		2%
15	Training					X			–
16	Works Inspection								–
17	Accessory/Audit	X	X						–
18	Civil Eng. Spec. Struc 1				X	X	X	X	–
19	Civil Eng. Buildings 2								–
20	Civil Eng. Public Roads 3				X	X	X	X	–
21	Territorial Planning				X	X	X	X	–
22	Energy 4				X	X	X	X	–
23	Engineering of Production Systems								–
	Total	1%	15%	71%	----	10%	2%	1%	100%

Figure 4.2 Matrix of the market segmentation of engineering services

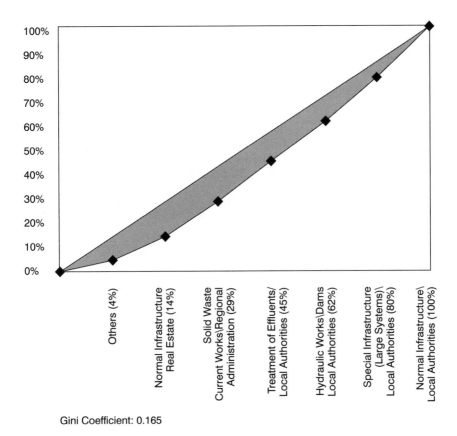

Gini Coefficient: 0.165

Figure 4.3 Concentration (distribution by segments)

The distribution of sales between the segments can be uniform or very unequal. A Lorenz curve can be used to evaluate this degree of concentration. The cumulative percentage of sales is plotted against one of the dimensions of the segmentation matrix or the segments in which the company is present (see Figure 4.3). That is, the variable on the x-axis can be any of the either two dimensions of the matrix (in this case, clients and services) or the actual segments. In any of the cases, the variables must be placed on the x-axis so that the Lorenz curve is always below the diagonal.

The behaviour of the Lorenz curve can be evaluated by the Gini coefficient (G), which varies between zero and one (see Figure 4.3). In the first case the distribution is equal (minimal concentration) and the Lorenz curve coincides with the bisector of the square. If the index has a value of one, the concentration is maximum and the Lorenz curve is asymptotic with reference to the x-axis. That is, when the concentration is very great

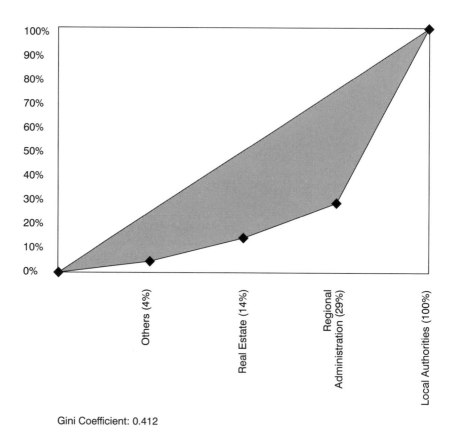

Gini Coefficient: 0.412

Figure 4.4 Concentration (distribution by clients)

something similar to the illustration in Figure 4.4 will be obtained. As the measurement of concentration is the shaded area above the triangle (southeastern part of the square), the Gini coefficient will approach its maximum value, which is 1.

When the concentration is minimal, the sales are proportionally distributed by clients and/or services and/or segments. Then the Lorenz curve practically coincides with the diagonal. The shaded zone is small and the ratio between this zone and the triangle (southeast of the square) is near zero (as the numerator is very small). This is the case of distribution by segments in Figure 4.3

In the example in question, (Figures 4.3, 4.4 and 4.5), the indices of concentration (Gini) are 0.165 for segments, 0.412 for clients and 0.2 for services.[3] The accumulated amounts corresponding to Figure 4.2 are on the x-axis. As the values of the index and behaviour of the curves do not have

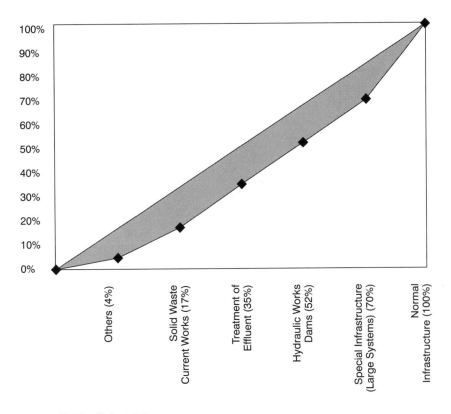

Gini Coefficient: 0.2

Figure 4.5 Concentration (distribution by services)

to be equal for clients, services and segments, there is an advantage in calculating the indices and curves for these three things separately, thus obtaining a *complete* view of the greater and lesser degree of the company's concentration of strategy.

Extension

Companies' strategies also vary in terms of their extension; that is, the percentage of industry covered. Here the Gini coefficient and the Lorenz graph can also be used but categories referring to the segments, clients and services in which the company is *not* present are also included on the x-axis (see Figure 4.6). That is, on the x-axis the exhaustive list of services, clients or segments of the matrix must be stated. There are six aspects worth noting about this calculation.

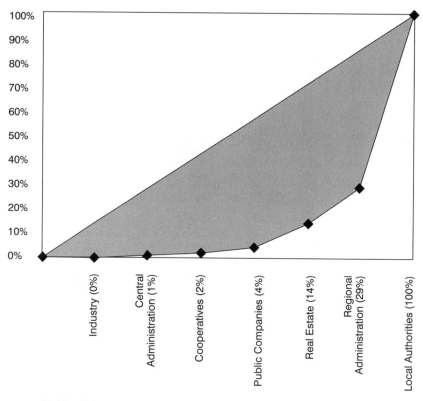

Gini Coefficient: 0.625
Extension: 0.375 (1 – Gini Coefficient)
Note: on the x-axis the numbers between brackets refer to accumulated values

Figure 4.6 Extension (Lorenz curve) by clients

First of all, the interpretation of the curve is similar to that made for the concentration concept, and in the examples in Figures 4.6 and 4.7, high arches (curves)[4] are recorded with a Gini coefficient of 0.625 in the case of distribution by type of clients, and this distribution is 0.765 per cent by type of services. In terms of clients, it should also be noted that in this example 3 of the 7 – regional administration, real estate and local authorities – 43 per cent represent 96 per cent of the invoicing. In terms of services, 5 of 23 (all types of infrastructures and treatment), which correspond to 22 in per cent, represent more than 96 per cent of the invoicing. That is:

			Variable Invoicing	
Clients	(3/7)	43 per cent	(ratio of 2.2)	96 per cent
Services	(5/23)	22 per cent	(ratio of 4.4)	96 per cent

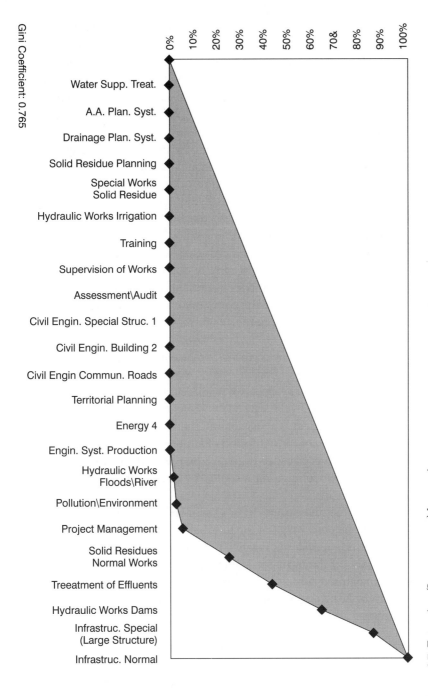

Gini Coefficient: 0.765

Figure 4.7 Extension (Lorenz curve) by services

Second, the segments variable should only be used on the x-axis when the total number of segments is relatively small. Otherwise it is preferable to use one of the two dimensions of the matrix (the x-axis or the ordinates, as done in Figures 4.6 and 4.7. Third, while it can be seen in the case of concentration that its measurement is given by the Gini coefficient, extension it is equal to one minus the Gini coefficient. That is, the extension (degree of cover of the industry) is so much the greater when the Lorenz curve is further from the diagonal, i.e., it is nearer zero.

In fourth place, it should be noted that the amounts of extension and concentration are not mathematically related, ie they are not one minus the other, as there is no comparison in the values of the x-axes. However, fifth, the Lorenz curve of extension is always equal or more curved (concave) than the concentration curve as the former contains as many or more zeros on the x-axis than the latter.[5]

In sixth place, an alternative evaluation of extension to the Gini coefficient (and Lorenz curve) would be simply obtained by using the ratio in which the numerator is the number of segments (or variables of one of the dimensions of the matrix) that the company occupies and the denominator is the total number of segments available. That is:

$$\frac{\text{Number the company occupies (of segments, clients or services)}}{\text{Total number available (of segments, clients or services)}}$$

Naturally this quotient is an easier and therefore less precise method of measuring the degree of the extension of strategy than the Gini coefficient and the Lorenz curve, because it gives equal weight to all the segments, regardless of the percentage represented by each in the company's total invoicing.

The most perfect measurement of extension would take into consideration not only the percentage of the total sales of the company which each segment, client or service represents, but also the relative weight of each in the total sales of the industry. Using such a measurement of extension, accuracy is acquired which is lost in simplicity and comparability with concentration. For these reasons this measurement is not used here but just mentioned.

Competitive position

A third strategic measurement is the company's strength of competitive position, which usually depends on its the market share. The evaluation of the market share always refers to a segment (and not to the industry)

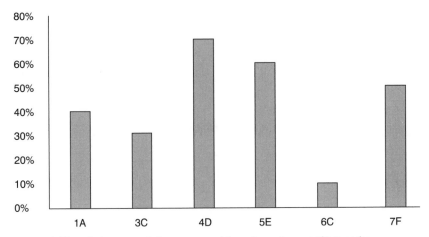

1. The whole segment, the average of three largest competitors or the average of all the competitors

Figure 4.8 Individual competitive position[1]

but the standard of comparison can vary between the total sales of the segment, the average sales of the three main competitors or the general average of competition in the segment. In general, it is useful to represent the competitive position of a company in a certain industry in terms of two bar charts (see Figures 4.8 and 4.9).

Figures 4.8 and 4.9 give examples of the representation of the competitive position of a company in the engineering services market. Figure 4.8 represents, segment by segment, the company's competitive position. Figure 4.9 illustrates this same competitive position, but in cumulative terms. Thus, the second column refers to segments 1A + 3C, the third to segments 1A + 3C + 4D, and so on.

The height of the bars in the cumulative graph follows two basic rules. First, as more segments are added, the height of the bars can never be greater than the maximum corresponding value up to that point in the individual competitive position graph (market share segment by segment). Second, the cumulative graph (Figure 4.9) does not vary in the same way as the individual competitive position graph (Figure 4.8), as the importance of the segments (in terms of sales volume) is variable. So, the height of each bar in the cumulative graph is in between the (smallest and greatest) heights of the bars to its left in the individual graph,[6] that is:

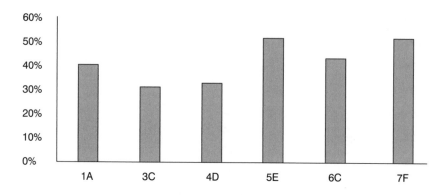

Figure 4.9 Cumulative competitive position

$$\text{smaller } AA \leq AC \geq \text{larger } AA$$

in which:

AC = height of the cumulative bar (Figure 4.9)
AA = height of the bar in the individual competitive position
(Figure 4.8)

There are four ways of evaluating the competitive position:

- simple (segment by segment);
- cumulative (all the segments);
- market share in absolute terms;
- market share in relative terms.

The *absolute* market share is the ratio of the sales of a company and the total of the market (or all the competition). The *relative* market share is the ratio of the sales of a company and the average market share of the three largest companies in the segment or the general average of its competition in the segment

Generally, the relative market share is a better indicator than the absolute market share as the competitive position of a company is different when it has, for example, 20 per cent of the market and the second, third and fourth largest competitors have 10 per cent, or when the second largest has 30 per cent, the third 25 per cent and the fourth 20 per cent.[7,8]

Diversity

Strategies can differ in terms of the diversity existing between the segments where the company is situated: that is, they can be more or less related (connected more or less in terms of the segmentation matrix).

If the segmentation matrix of an industry is well drawn, the nearer the two segments are to one another the more similar they are, and the diversity between them is less. Thus, for simplicity let us say that as diversity increases identically across the two dimensions of the segmentation matrix, the diversity between segments can be evaluated by the number of segments existing between them.

As an example let us take the case of the segmentation matrix of the retail bank already used in Chapter 2. Thus in Figure 4.10 the diversity between the two segments 1A and 1B is one; between 1A and 2B it is two; between 2B and 4C2 it is four; and so on. Two evaluations can be made. The first is the average diversity of each segment in which the company is (which is the average of the diversity of each segment in relation to all the others in which the company is situated). The second is the average diversity of the strategy (which is the average of the average diversity of all the segments). Both measurements vary in accordance with the segments in which the company is if they are all accumulated in one sole area of the matrix or scattered in various zones of the segmentation matrix. The greater the diversity the less synergy.

Let us suppose that in the matrix in Figure 4.10 a company occupies three segments: 1A, 2B and 4C2. The average diversity of segment 1A is:

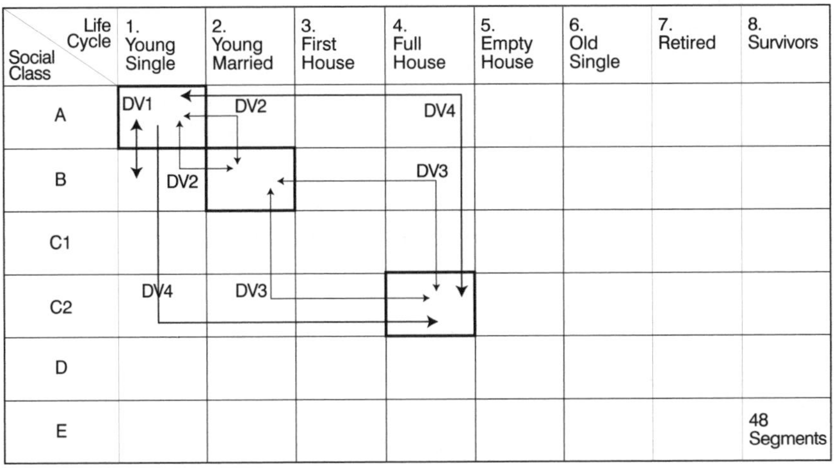

Social Class \ Life Cycle	1. Young Single	2. Young Married	3. First House	4. Full House	5. Empty House	6. Old Single	7. Retired	8. Survivors
A	DV1	DV2		DV4				
B	DV2			DV3				
C1								
C2	DV4	DV3						
D								
E								48 Segments

DV1 A difference of one in the diversity between segments 1A and 1B
DV2 A difference of one in the diversity between segments 1A and 2B
DV3 A difference of one in the diversity between segments 2B and 4C2
DV1 A difference of one in the diversity between segments 1A and 4C2

Figure 4.10 Examples of diversity in the segmentation matrix of a retail bank

Diversity of 1A in relation to 2B = 2
Diversity of 1A in relation to 4C2 = 6
(2 + 6)/2 = 4 (average diversity of segment 1A)

Similarly, the average diversity of segment 2B is:
Diversity in relation to segment 1A = 2
Diversity in relation to segment 4C2 = 4
(2 + 4)/2 = 3 (average diversity of segment 2B)

Finally, the average diversity of segment 4C2 is:
Diversity in relation to segment 1A = 6
Diversity in relation to segment 2B = 4
(6 + 4)/2 = 5 (average diversity of segment 4C2)

Therefore the average diversity of the company's strategy in the industry, is:

(4 + 3 + 5)/3 = 13/8.3 = 4.3

(which is the average of the average diversity of the three segments which the company occupies).

Standardizing the diversity

While concentration and extension vary between zero and one and the competitive position can acquire values between zero and 100 per cent, the variation interval of the diversity fluctuates in accordance with the number of segments existing in the industry. The maximum diversity occurs when two segments are in opposite corners of the segmentation matrix, in which case the diversity is equal to the sum of the number lines minus one with the number of columns minus one. That is:

$$1 \le \text{Diversity} \ge (\text{maximum no. of lines} - 1) + (\text{maximum no. of columns} - 1)[9]$$

In order to standardize the value of the diversity, put it as varying between zero and one or between zero and 100 per cent (ie like the concentration, extension and competitive position). The value of the diversity can be divided by the maximum value it can have (no. lines + no. columns - 2) and therefore we have:

$$\frac{D}{n + m - 2} \times 100$$

Characteristic / Type of measure	1. Measurable by	2. Alternative Units		3. Total of the Calculation Methods (1×2)	4. Variation Interval
Concentration	–GINI ratio (LORENZ Curve)	– Segments – One dimension of the matrix – Another dimension of the matrix		Three	0 – 1
Extension	– GINI ratio (LORENZ Curve); or – Quotient (between where it is and the total)	– Segments – One dimension of the matrix – Another dimension of the matrix		Six	0 – 1
Competitive Position	Bar Graphic	Simple	Absolute Relative	Four	0 – 1
		Cumu-lative	Absolute Relative		
Diversity	Ratio	Absolute Relative		Two	0 – 1*

* In the case of the relative measure

Figure 4.11 Synthesis

in which n = no. of lines and m = no. of columns; the ratio varies between zero and 100 per cent.

Synthesis

Figure 4.11 summarizes the analysis up to this point. Until now it has focused on four variables of strategy: concentration, extension, competitive position and diversity. Concentration is measured by the Gini coefficient and the Lorenz curve. Extension can be evaluated by the same method or also by a simple ratio of the areas covered in relation to the total number of areas. In concentration or extension, the segments or one of the two dimensions of the segmentation matrix can be used in the x-axis.

There are four possible ways of evaluating the competitive position (see Figure 4.11). There are two in which to evaluate the diversity: the average diversity between segments in absolute terms or in relative terms to the maximum value of the diversity. For all evaluations, the coefficient of the variation is between zero (minimum) and one (maximum). In the next section let us see how these concepts can be represented graphically and the conclusions to be reached from the values they assume, that is, *the use of evaluating the strategy.*

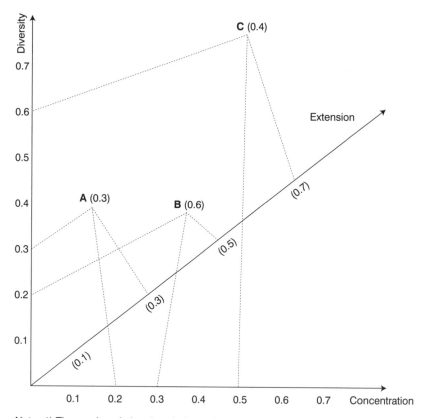

Note: 1) The numbers in brackets indicate the company's competitive position.
2) Its position in the three axes corresponds to the value of the diversity, extension and concentration of its strategy.

Figure 4.12 Visualization of strategy

THE ADVANTAGES OF QUANTIFYING STRATEGY

The first advantage of quantifying strategy is that after quantification the position of a company can be visualized in three dimensions (diversity, extension and concentration), as shown in Figure 4.12. The value in brackets shows its competitive position. Thus for example company A has 0.2 of concentration (20 per cent); 0.3 of extension (30 per cent); and 0.3 of diversity (30 per cent). Its competitive position is 0.3 (30 per cent).

Company B already has reduced diversity (0.2) but greater concentration (0.3) and much greater extension (0.5). Its competitive position is

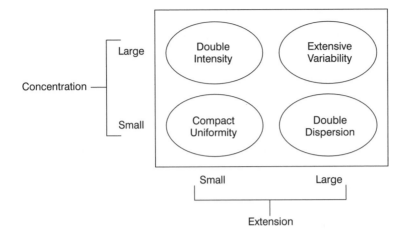

1. **Double Intensity** – A small percentage of the company's segments do not only represent a large part of its sales but also a small part of the industry's total.

2. **Compact Uniformity** – The company's sales are distributed uniformly by its segments but they represent a small portion of the industry.

3. **Double Dispersion** – The company disperses its sales uniformly in many segments and these represent a large area of the industry.

4. **Extension Variability** – The company is present in many segments but unequally (concentrates its sales in few).

Figure 4.13 The four extreme cases in terms of concentration and extension

much superior (0.6). Finally company C presents values of 0.6, 0.7 and 0.5. Its competitive position is 0.4.

Another way of visualizing the strategy of a company is by using a Cartesian graph in which any of the four evaluations for the two dimensions of the graph can be chosen. For example, using the dimensions concentration and extension four extreme situations are obtained. One strategy is twice as intense when its extension is small (the company is in a small part of the industry), and its concentration is large (even in the few segments in which it is, the company concentrates its sales in a reduced percentage of them). The opposite (double dispersion) relates to a company covering a large part of the industry and having its sales distributed uniformly in the segments in which it is present, and so on (see Figure 4.13).

The second advantage of evaluating strategy is that much information

Characteristics of the measurements
1.   Statistics (non-dynamic)
2.   Industry to industry (refers to the strategy of a company in an industry)

Advantage
1.   Summarizes/abridges
    1.1   For us
    1.2   For other members of the institution
    1.3   For third parties

Our strategy (if we can give something a number it means that we know something about that thing)

2.   Therefore
    2.1   It transmits more information
    2.2   More precisely
    2.3   With less effort
    2.4   In less time

Example / Variable	One	Two	Three	Four
Concentration	0.8	0.4	0.2	0.2
Extension	0.2	0.5	0.7	0.7
Competitive Position	0.6	0.6	0.6	0.2
Diversity	0.1	0.1	0.3	0.8
Commentary Position	Large concentration and small extension and strong competitive position	Company covering 50% of the industry but with more evenly distributed sales and strong competitive position	Company with evenly distributed sales, covering a large part of the industry with strong competitive position	Great uniformity, large coverage of the industry, diversity and weak competitive position

Figure 4.14 Examples of synthesis

about the strategy can be summarized for us, for other members of the institution and third parties. Let us suppose we want to describe the strategy we want to implement (or its present strategy) to another person inside or outside our company. Without quantification we would say: 'Well, we have covered a vast area of industry, our sales are distributed in a fairly equal way in the segments in which we are present, our diversity is small and the competitive position strong.' That would take more than thirty words. We would have transmitted more information, more precisely, with less effort and we would have saved time if we had said that this strategy is: extension – 0.6; concentration – 0.5; diversity – 0.1 and competitive position – 0.7. Our interlocutor would have learnt much more about the strategy if we had talked less. It should be added that quantification of strategy is also useful for us as it also allows us to fix and determine ideas. Figure 4.14 gives other examples of the power of synthesis and elucidation in quantifying strategy.[10]

The third advantage of quantifying the present strategy of a company is that by doing so conclusions are immediately obtained regarding strategic alterations to be implemented. That is, the quantification of the present strategy acts as an indication of the strategy to be followed. It clearly indicates[11] what to alter and what to keep.

For this purpose, as shown in Figure 4.15, the methodology starts from three basic prerequisites. First, the competitive position is all the greater: with greater the synergy, and the more the strong points are equal to the critical factors of success.

On the other hand, synergy is all the greater when the diversity is less (as this is inversely linked to relatedness between the segments). Finally, it is to be expected that the degree of proximity between critical factors of success and strong points increases with concentration and diminishes with extension. The basic principle is that of concentration of strengths, as stated by Clausewitz: 'to be strong in one way in a few places and not weak in any way in many places'. Or, as Mao Tse-Tung said: 'I have ten against a hundred, but I always fight ten against one, one hundred times, and like that I win.' These suppositions imply that the probability of being in a good competitive position is all the greater when there is *less* diversity, less extension and greater *concentration* (see Figure 4.15).[12] That means if a company has a strong competitive position and large diversity, great extension and little concentration, this occurs in spite of that diversity, extension and concentration and not due to them.

Three schemes are now presented, of which Figure 4.16 shows the simplest. Based on the values assumed by the diversity, extension and concentration of a company it is now possible immediately to draw strategic recommendations, using only two variables: competitive position and diversity.

Therefore the situation of large diversity and weak competitive position (D in Figure 4.16) suggests the need for a strategy of reduction of the diversity (concentration) so as to increase the synergy between them and thus to strengthen the competitive position. In situation C in Figure 4.16, there is weak competitiveness in spite of little diversity (therefore, in theory, the synergy is great). A company which is in this situation must consider changing to another segment, preferably of the same industry, or

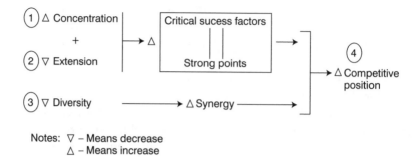

Notes: ▽ – Means decrease
        △ – Means increase

Figure 4.15 Basic prerequisites of strategic recommendations based on quantification

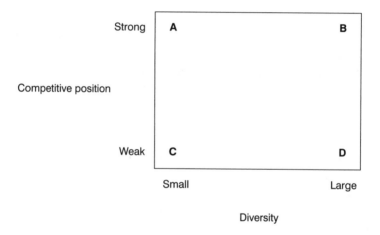

Figure 4.16 Combining the measurements of competitive position and diversity

withdrawing from the present one(s). In situation A, the company can look for synergetic segments in order to expand its activity. In that case, the extension will increase and probably the concentration will decrease. Finally, in situation B, the appropriate strategy is that of maintenance. Figure 4.17 summarizes the strategic implications of these four situations.

Figure 4.18 shows a more complex typology of recommendations (according to the level of complexity). Two important types of situations can be seen: when the competitive position is strong (in which it is possible either to opt for obtaining the benefits of the actual situation – in terms of profit and cash-flow – or to use these benefits to obtain new opportunities).

When the competitive situation is weak, two situations must be distinguished: when something remedial can be done by adjusting the

Situation / Strategic reply	A	B	C	D
Expansion	✓			
Maintenance		✓		
Change			✓	
Concentration				✓

Figure 4.17 The relationship between situations and strategic responses

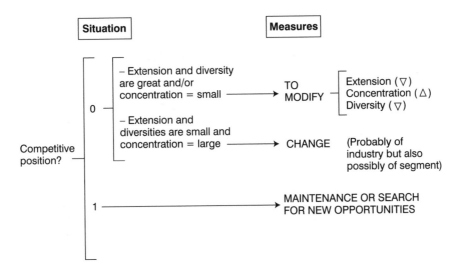

Notes: The values from 0 to 1 should be read near to 0 or to 1,
that is weak or strong (small or large)

▽ – Means diminish
△ – Means increase

Figure 4.18 Typology of recommendations

extension, concentration and diversity (reducing the first and/or increasing the second and/or decreasing the third); and when nothing can be done in this area (as the diversity is already low, the extension reduced and concentration high), a situation in which purely and simply the only option is change (probably of industry or possibly just of segment(s) within the industry).

Thus, as a result of the values assumed by competitive position, concentration, extension and diversity, eight alternative recommenda-

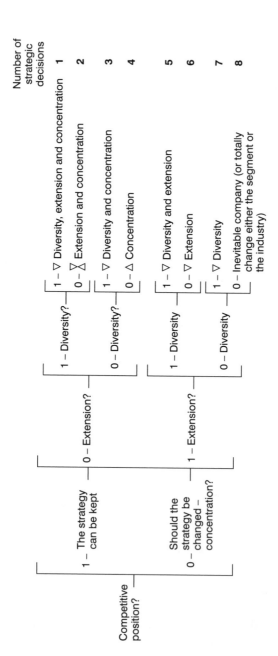

Figure 4.19 Extended typology of recommendations

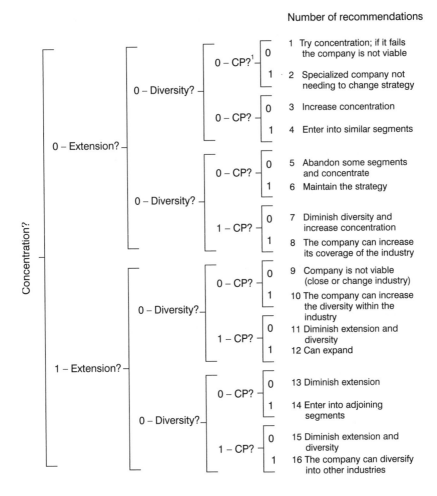

Number of recommendations

1 Try concentration; if it fails the company is not viable

2 Specialized company not needing to change strategy

3 Increase concentration

4 Enter into similar segments

5 Abandon some segments and concentrate

6 Maintain the strategy

7 Diminish diversity and increase concentration

8 The company can increase its coverage of the industry

9 Company is not viable (close or change industry)

10 The company can increase the diversity within the industry

11 Diminish extension and diversity

12 Can expand

13 Diminish extension

14 Enter into adjoining segments

15 Diminish extension and diversity

16 The company can diversify into other industries

1. in segments where concentration occurs, the competitive position improves

Figure 4.20 Typology of strategic recommendations

tions can be obtained, as shown in Figure 4.19. For example, if the competitive position is weak, the concentration great, the extension small and the diversity large, it is logical that this last variable has to be reduced in order to improve the competitive position – situation 7 in Figure 4.19. In another situation, if the competitive position is weak, the diversity and extension are small but the concentration small, the concentration must be increased (recommendation 4), and so on.

Figure 4.20 shows the most complex typology with 16 recommendations, in accordance with the values assumed by the concentration, extension, diversity and competitive position. For example, if the extension, concentration, diversity and competitive position are weak, the first thing to be done is adjust (increasing the variable concentration) – situation 1. In situation 3, in which the diversity, extension, competitive position and concentration are weak, the last must be increased. Situation 9 deals with an unprofitable company in the actual segments of the industry where it is and therefore must simply cease activity or change industry, etc.

These three typologies (Figures 4.18, 4.19 and 4.20) of increasing complexity are all based on the quantification of strategy and on the same four variables: concentration, extension, diversity and competitive position. That is one of the advantages of making the quantification.

CONCLUSION

This chapter has presented four dimensions of measuring the strategy of a company in an industry (extension, concentration, competitive position and diversity). Three advantages result from these measurements: first, the possibility of preparing graphs enabling the present or intended strategy of the company to be visualized (Figures 4.12 and 4.13). Second, by quantifying strategy much more information is given in a much simpler way than by mere description in words of this strategy (Figure 4.14). Finally, the quantification of strategy means conclusions can be immediately drawn about the strategy to follow, as clear and simple recommendations can be obtained (Figures 4.16–4.20). In this way, quantification of the present strategy allows the extraction of suggestions and the alterations to be made.

Visualization, information and strategic conclusions are the outputs of this chapter, the outputs of quantifying strategy. The next chapter is dedicated to *qualifying* strategy.

5

Qualifying
strategy

M Porter   Karl von Clausewitz

INTRODUCTION

In the previous chapter, strategy was quantified. In the present one, it will
be *qualified*. Both quantification and qualification contribute to measuring
strategy. With regard to qualification, any company in any industry can
follow one of four types of strategies and opt among being: *a lion, a horse,
a mink or a lynx*. This choice is *independent* of the type of industry and the
number of segments in it. It is *dependent* upon how the company competes
(in quality, cost, delivery, etc) and the number of segments it targets. Let's
see why.

The worst strategic error is to be stuck in the middle.
To not be willing to choose which of these routes
to competitive advantage the company is going to follow:
to worry about quality and differentiation
but not to achieve uniqueness in anything;
and to think about segmentation of the market,
but to not dedicate themselves to a particular narrow segment.

M PORTER

Strategy is to decide where to be and with what strength.

KARL VON CLAUSEWITZ

After quantifying strategy the question arises as to whether it is also possible to qualify it, that is, to give it a name, to typify the strategy of a company in whatever industry it might be. The question is not easy to answer, given that, as illustrated in Figure 5.1, an institution within an industry can follow a very great number of strategies. It can occupy any number of segments, or any combination of segments. The possible combinations are numerous. For M segments in an industry there are:

$$M + C^M_2 + C^M_3 + \dots$$
$$C^M_{M-1} + C^M_M$$

possible strategies, in which C^M_i denotes the combination of C and M given by the mathematical formula

$$C_i = \frac{M}{i! \, (M-i)}$$

The total number of possible strategies is:

$$M + C^M_2 + C^M_3 +$$
$$C^M_4 \dots C^M_{M-1} +$$
$$C^M_M$$

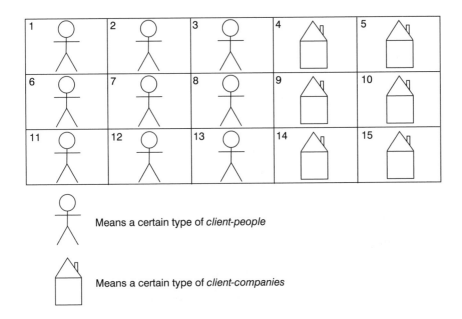

Means a certain type of *client-people*

Means a certain type of *client-companies*

Figure 5.1 The numerous strategies of an institution within an industry

There are 13 strategies that are obviously possible in an industry that occupies four segments. The question is: In spite of the large variety of possible strategies in an industry can they be classified in a simple typology? Can we typify them? The answer is yes. The simplest typology is that of Nelson Valverde,[1] which differentiates between four large categories of strategy: mink, lion, lynx and horse (see Figure 5.2).

NELSON VALVERDE'S TYPOLOGY

This typology is made up of a matrix in which the dimensions are: the proportion of available segments occupied by the institution (a maximum of all those of the industry and a minimum of one); and whether competition is undertaken on the basis of price/cost or not. If so, a company can compete on the basis either of quality – whatever may be understood by quality (durability, comfort, design, size, facility of use, precision, etc) – or delivery (rapidity, quantity or time). Thus there are *four large types of possible strategies*. Whatever the strategy followed by an institution in an industry may be, it can be classified as one of these four types. Figure 5.2 gives four examples for financial services: Morgan Guarantee Trust

Implications of the positions of the matrix

Strategy
Mink (few segments, high added value)
Morgan

1. Sophisticated products/adapted to a certain segment.
2. *Marketing* adapted to each segment.
3. Image of speciality/exclusiveness.

Lion (many segments and high added value)
American Express

1. Sophisticated product/adapted to a certain segment.
2. *Marketing* adapted to each segment.
3. Image of leader.
4. Larger number of segment than mink.

Horse (many segments and little added value)
Prudential

1. Less sophisticated product than lion.
2. Fewer models than lion.
3. Image of good purchase/appropriate.
4. Wagers on progressive economies.
5. Institutional marketing.

Lynx (few segments and high added value)
Trustee Savings Bank

1. Less sophisticated products than lion.
2. Fewer segments and models than lion.
3. Image of good purchase/appropriate.
4. Little service, smaller price margin.
5. Fewer segments than horse.

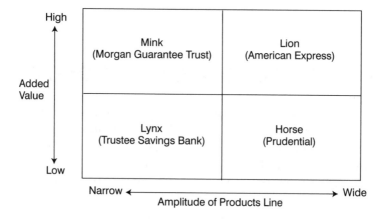

Figure 5.2 Nelson Valverde's typology

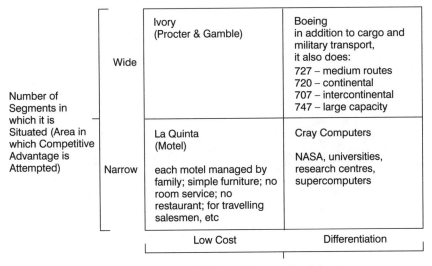

Figure 5.3 Strategic options according to Nelson Valverde

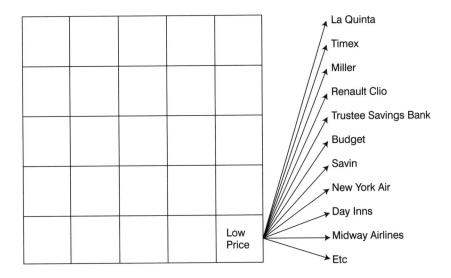

Figure 5.4 The lynx strategy

Houses and schools	Small Companies and Liberal Professionals	Large and Medium-sized Companies	Scientific and Military Institutions	
1	2	5		Micros
	3	6		Supermicros
	4	7		Minis
		8		Superminis
		9		Mainframes
			10	Minisuper
			11 CRAY	Supercomputers

Figure 5.5 Cray Computers as an example of the mink strategy

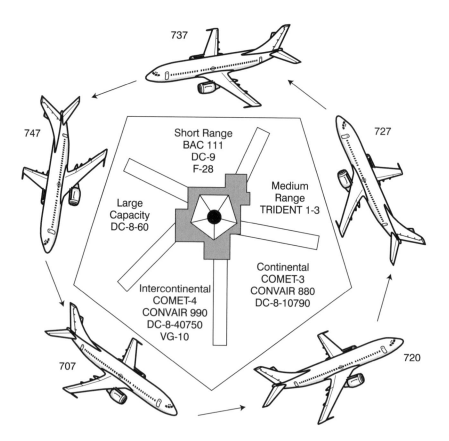

Figure 5.6 Boeing's lion strategy

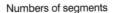

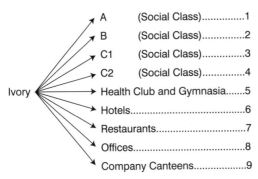

Figure 5.7 Ivory's horse strategy

(mink); American Express (lion); Prudential (horse) and Trustee Savings Bank (lynx).

A *lynx* is a company specializing in one or few market segments and competes on the basis of *price/cost*. It is a company specializing in the lower end of the market. This is the case with the La Quinta motels (see Figure 5.3). La Quinta is a motel chain like Holiday Inn, but specialized in clients in terms of price. That is the reason why the hotels are managed by a family; there is no room service (just a mini-bar); there are no restaurants (to overcome this inconvenience the La Quinta motels are usually situated facing a restaurant that is open 24 hours or a large part of the day); and the bedroom furniture is simple. It is a clean, simple and cheap motel, of which travelling salesmen, medical representatives and other kinds of travellers are the main clients.[2] In every industry there are companies specializing in the lynx strategy, for example: Budget (renting cars), Savin (photocopiers), all low-range cars (Renault Clio, etc), Miller in beers, Timex for watches, etc (see Figure 5.4).

A *mink company* is the extreme opposite of a lynx, and is illustrated in Figure 5.2 by Morgan, and in Figures 5.5 by Cray Computers. It is a strategy characterized by occupation of few segments (like the lynx); but in which the company competes based on quality or delivery (not price). As shown in Figure 5.5, within the 11 available possible segments of the computer industry, Cray Computers specializes in one: the production of supercomputers, which it sells to NASA, research centres and universities. As the sale of these supercomputers is based not on price but on quality (capacity, rapidity of processing and adaptation to the specific needs of the client) this is a mink strategy.

Both the lynx and the mink have one fact in common: such companies specialize in few segments. The *lion* occupies all available segments, and has a model for each one. The *horse* produces fewer models than the number of segments it occupies.

The lion's strategy is illustrated in Figure 5.2 by American Express and in Figures 5.3 and 5.6 by Boeing. Basically the company occupies many segments and offers an intrinsically different model for each segment: the Boeing 737 for short distance flights, the Boeing 747 for large capacity, the 707 for intercontinental flights, the 720 for continental flights and so on. The competitors vary in each segment – see Figure 5.4.

Coca-Cola in soft drinks and Vlasic Food in pickles are also examples of lion strategies. Coca-Cola has an intrinsic differentiated product (a model) for each market segment. It has the classic coke; the new coke; the tab; the caffeine-free; etc. Then, the caffeine-free can be new or classic or diet, etc. Similarly the pickles market in the United States was initially dominated by Heinz and Del Monte,[3] who distributed the same product in all the regions of the United States until Vlasic started a process of purchase of regional makes, each of which was adapted to the local taste. Today Heinz has 10 per cent and Vlasic 26 per cent of the US market share.

While the lion strategy has a one-to-one relationship between segments and models, the horse strategy is to opt to serve many segments but, to maximize economies of scale, to do it with few models. So the number of models is fewer than the number of segments they serve. One example is the soap Ivory (see Figures 5.3 and 5.7), which without great variations (except for the packaging, colour and distribution channels) serves segments A, B, C1, C2, gymnasia and health clubs, hotels, restaurants, offices and company canteens.[4]

Other examples of users of the horse strategy are Black & Decker and Texas Instruments. Although there are other more sophisticated makes adapted to each segment, the Black & Decker basic model serves several segments of the DIY industry without great alterations (professionals, hobbyists, individuals, offices, etc). In the same manner, Texas Instruments makes fewer models than the number of segments it serves (small-size, low-price desk calculator; calculator for complex operations; etc).[5]

A smaller number of models than segments, global institutional marketing, groups of models and a good price for each model due to economies of scale and/or fewer direct costs are the characteristics of the horse strategy. Table 5.1 presents several examples of lynx, mink, horses and lions. It is possible to find examples of these four basic types of strategy in all industries.

Table 5.1 Examples of lynx, mink, horses and lions

Lynx	Mink	Horses	Lions
Trustee Savings	Morgan	Prudential	American
Bank	Bentley	McDonalds	Express
Renault Clio	Chivas Regal	Sears	Banco Comercial
Timex	La Tour d'Argent	Ivory	Português
Savin	Steinway	Black & Decker	Boeing
La Quinta	Patek Philippe	Heinz (pickles)	Coca-Cola
Day Inns	Häagen-Dazs	Del Monte	Vlasic Foods
New York Air	Food Emporium	(pickles)	(pickles)
Midway Airlines	Byerly's	Texas Instruments	Citibank
Budget	Calvin Klein	Wrangler	Exxon (Office
Miller	Jordache	Levis	Automation)
Fiat Punto	Michelob	Briggs & Stretton	IBM
		Lincoln Electric	Unisys
			Honda
			Xerox

SIX IMPORTANT ASPECTS OF QUALIFICATION

Having arrived here, it is important to note six aspects of qualification. First, any industry can be seen in terms of four extreme opposites. The lynx is the opposite of the lion (price versus quality; small number of segments versus large number). The mink (few segments and quality) is the opposite of the horse (many segments and wagers on low cost/price through economies of scale). This is shown in Figure 5.8, which compares McDonalds (horse), with the Parisian restaurant La Tour d'Argent (mink). The mink and lynx companies fish with a rod, while horses and lions use a net (and everything that enters the net ... is fish).

Second, it should be pointed out that there is no strategy more difficult than that of the lion. A company which follows this strategy wants to be in a differentiated way in many (eventually in all) of the segments of its industry. That implies the company recognizes that:

1   all the segments are sufficiently attractive in terms of size, profit margin and attractiveness;

2   synergy exists between them;

3   although the critical factors of success vary from segment to segment,[5] the company considers it has strong points in all of them and therefore competitive advantage;

4   the company has sufficient resources to be in many segments at the same time.

As can be seen, the lion is a strategy of great courage and the name 'lion' is appropriate. The necessary courage (points 1, 2, 3 and 4 above) is so difficult and great that even large companies fail at times to implement it. Exxon tried to encircle IBM and Xerox in the office automation industry and failed.

The third aspect worth noting is a question that everyone should ask at the very beginning. The strategy of the lion can be understood (one segment, one model). But how is it possible to implement the strategy of the horse, which has one or few models to serve many market segments? Basically they want to have their cake and eat it at the same time. That is, they want to attract various types of clients (everything which comes into the net is welcome...) and not sacrifice economies of scale by differentiation.[6] The question is: How is that possible? As Figures 5.9 and 5.10 show, the reply must be found in the concept of the offer used in marketing. This concept contains all the aspects regarding the introduction of a product on the market.

A distinction must be made between who introduces (sources of information and persuasion) and what is introduced. With reference to what is introduced, a distinction must be made between 'what' –the fundamental core, and what is in the product – and accessory and intangible aspects. Essential aspects and the core are the parts and components of the product, its texture (comfort), durability, colour (dyeing and printing), size (capacity), etc. Accessory aspects are the name (make), design, packaging, wrapping and delivery quantities, and other characteristics such as security systems. Intangible aspects are the image, service (installation, practice and repairs), guarantee, distribution channels (place, time and rapidity) and price (amount and payment conditions).

Models can be differentiated by not intrinsic (core) aspects but based on accessory and intangible aspects or, if another classification is preferred, based on the non-essential *what*, where, when, how much and how. Fifteen elements are presented in Figures 5.9 and 5.10, so readers can adopt those that they find more useful in reference terms.

In spite of serving nine different segments (see Figure 5.7) that is how Ivory managed with a product whose size, intrinsic contents and perfume

1. Not very Sophisticated Product – Easy to Understand
2. Economies in Size – Automatization – Have it your way (No Frills)
3. Little Service and Information (Counters = Self Service)
4. Low Price/Margin
5. Mass-marketing Channels

Comparative Advantage

1. Very Sophisticated French Cusine, Difficult to Understand
   (Employees help to explain the menu)
2. Personalized Meal
   (Garnishes with each dish, well done, underdone, etc)
3. A Lot of Service, Large Team of Specialized Employees
   for wines, desserts, main course
4. Luxurious Decoration
5. High Price/Margin
6. Spcialized Marketing Channels
   (magazines, sponsors, etc)

Figure 5.8 The horse compared with the mink

remain the same and of which the only variations are with packaging, colour, distribution channels and sales force. In the same way, Black & Decker has fewer models than the segments it serves, using accessories (name, packaging, design, wrapping) and intangibles (image, service, guarantee, distribution channels) to differentiate between the various models. Although this suggestion is somewhat exaggerated, it is a little like the military cook who was asked what was for lunch. He replied, 'For the officers' mess, Hungarian goulash; for the sergeants' mess, veal *à la jardinière*; for the soldiers' mess, stew with potatoes.'

The fourth aspect worth noting is that as the lion's strategy is the most demanding (it implies being in many segment differentiating not only the accessory and intangible aspects but also the intrinsic ones), the present world tendency, called *transnational competition*, helps to implement it. Formerly, reasons for *vertical integration* prevailed for the productive

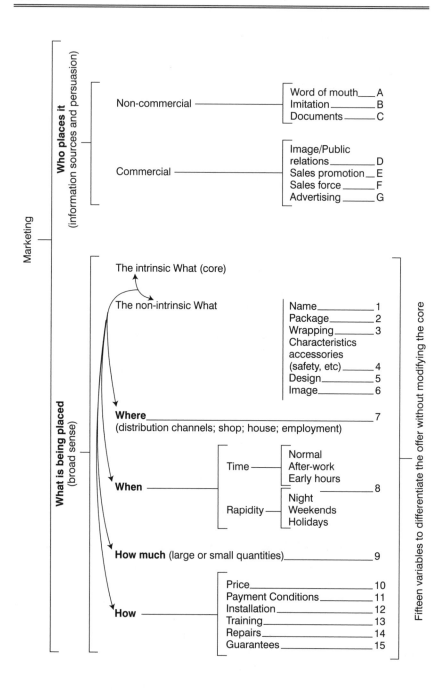

Figure 5.9 The concept of offer in marketing essential aspects

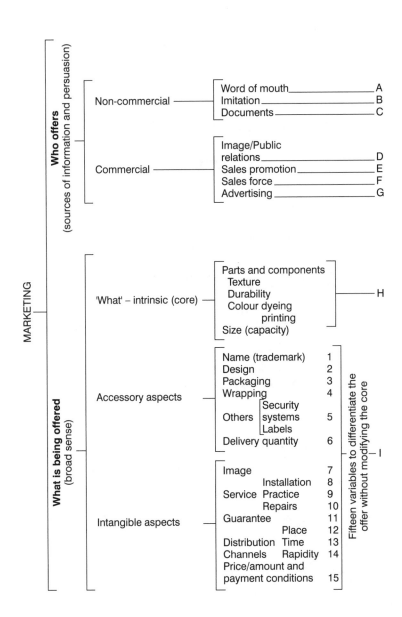

Figure 5.10 The concept of offer in marketing (accessory and intangible aspects)

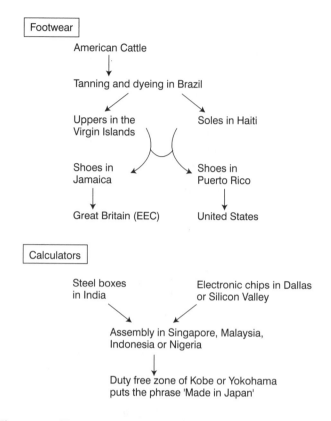

Figure 5.11 Transnational assembly

process in *just one* geographic zone (facility of coordination, lower transport costs, handling and saving of energy due to proximity). Nowadays with the tendencies for:

- reduction in transport costs (maritime, air, railway);
- improvement in communications (express mail, fax, video conferences);
- dismantling of customs barriers (duties, quotas and technical barriers);

the tendency is vertically to dismantle the productive process by various geographical areas. That is, a product is divided into parts and the production of each part is assigned to a more appropriate area of the globe for cost reasons: labour; possibilities of obtaining economies of scale; proximity to the final market; existence of certain raw materials; lenient environmental law (eg important in the case of tanning and dyeing which are highly polluting tasks); know-how of the labour force; climate, etc.

Figure 5.11 gives two examples referring to footwear and calculators. Footwear sold in the United States and Great Britain starts its production in cattle breeding (which in general is in the US). Tanning and dyeing are done in Brazil (the first task is labour intensive and both pollute); the vamp (top part of the shoe) is made in the Virgin Islands and the soles in Haiti. The shoes are then hand or machine sewn, according to the segment to which they are assigned – higher or lower – in Jamaica or Puerto Rico as the former country has preferential access to Great Britain (and therefore the EEC) and the second to the United States.

Nowadays the use of calculators is universal. Many of them have 'Made in Japan' written on their packaging. If readers turn over their own calculators, they will probably find this phrase written on the back. It so happens that in some cases the Japanese content of the calculators is rather limited... Let us have a look. The steel boxes are made in India; the electronic chips in Dallas or Silicon Valley. They are assembled in Singapore, Malaysia, Indonesia or Nigeria; then the calculators go to a Japanese free port such as Kobe or Yokohama, where they receive the Japanese added value: that is, the phrase 'Made in Japan' is written on them (see Figure 5.11). The same process occurs in a large variety of industries, such as car components, garments, textiles, footwear, furniture, tyres, cash registers, turbines, tractors, laboratory instruments, dialysis machines, refrigerators and other domestic appliances, the manufacture of bicycles and motorcycles, etc.

An interesting question is: What is the relationship of the vertical disintegration with the four basic types of strategy developed above? Briefly, vertical disintegration on the geographical level (global), also known as transnational competition, allows a company to implement a lion strategy in a certain geographic zone more easily (in contrast to the horse); and to be a lion (enter) in more segments as it is possible to out-source more parts of the model, thus differentiating it even more.

This leads us to the fifth aspect worthy of note, which is: When should a company follow a lion strategy and when a horse strategy?

Figure 5.12 summarizes the characteristics of the horse strategy and compares its advantages with those of the lion strategy.[7] Basically, in the choice between one and the other a comparison must be made of: what is won in economies of scale; whether the savings in direct costs compensate; and the lower value given the client with the correspondingly lower price which can be asked. After comparison, the decision can be made as to whether the company should enter a new segment with the strategy of the lion or the horse (with regard to the segments in which it is already present). That depends on:

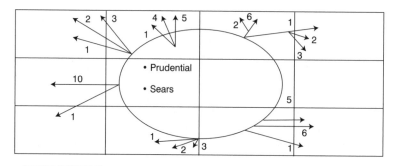

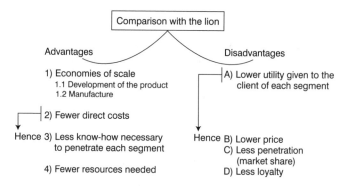

Figure 5.12 The horse strategy

1   the existence or not of competitors, specialized in the various market segments;

2   the importance of economies of scale;

3   the number of existing clients who consider price (economies of scale) and value (differentiation) to be important.

THE RELATIONSHIP BETWEEN QUANTITATIVE AND QUALITATIVE MEASURES OF STRATEGY

The previous chapter developed four quantitative measures of strategy: concentration, extension, competitiveness and diversity. This chapter has presented four qualitative measures: lynx, mink, lion and horse. The question arises as to how they relate to one another. In order to make a long answer short, this should be stated as follows:

1   A lynx or a mink company is usually characterized by low extension and (to a certain extent) high concentration; there is therefore a positive correlation between these four (2 plus 2) measures.[8]

2   Lions and horses rate high in extension and (usually) low in concentration.

3   Diversity tends to be higher with lions and horses than with lynxes and mink.

4   Competitiveness (measured through market share) usually bears no correlation with any of the four qualitative measures.[9, 10]

This chapter classified the various types of strategy which an institution can follow. In Chapter 6 an analysis will be made of how to summarize strategy.

6

Summarizing strategy

T Levitt

INTRODUCTION

Having qualified and quantified strategy in the previous two chapters, the present one will *synthesize* it; that is, it will indicate how to summarize a firm's strategy by indicating its *mission*, its *raison d'être*, how it makes a living, what its business is. That is done by a short, simple phrase, capturing the essence of the position of the company on the market, such as: leisure is our business (Yamaha); toilet products (Johnson & Johnson); babies are our business (Gerber); foot comfort in the United States (Scholl); boats in France (Beneteau) and so on.

The advantage of defining the mission is that by summarizing the strategy and capturing its essence in a simple phrase, a *focal point* is obtained. This aids concentration of effort and clarity of objectives for everyone from the leader of the company to the workforce.

> *If any road is okay, the chief executive might as well pack his attaché case and go fishing. If an organization does not know or care where it is going, it does not need to advertise that fact with a ceremonial figurehead. Everybody will notice it soon enough.*
>
> THEODORE LEVITT IN MARKETING MYOPIA

THE IMPORTANCE OF DEFINING THE MISSION

First of all in the previous chapters the strategic plan was prepared (ie the strategy was defined), then it was quantified (ie the strategy was evaluated), and in Chapter 5, strategy was qualified. Now it would be good if the strategy could be synthesized capturing its essence in a phrase: what is our business? How does the company earn its living?

If that was possible then it would produce:

1   Definition (Chapter 3)

2   Quantification (Chapter 4)

3   Qualification (Chapter 5)

4   Synthesis (Chapter 6).

Those four elements together would form the focal point – for concentration of effort and clarity of objectives – for everyone from the head of the company down through the entire staff. For this purpose it is necessary to have a short simple phrase which captures the essence of the company's position in the market, defining its business. How can it be done? How can the strategy be thus synthesized?

It is very important to do it well, for several reasons. First of all because an institution's mission is never obvious. In the definition of mission, common expressions as to how the institution intends to make money, obtain profits or grow should not be used. As mentioned in Chapter 3, that is the same as someone saying they want to be happy. In its definition, the institution needs to show what it is going to do in order to be happy – what its business is, what its activity is, how it earns its living.

The second reason why the definition of mission is never obvious is that a small alteration in it is capable of totally changing the prospects of the company. This is illustrated by the story which supposedly happened to André Heiniger, chairman of Rolex. One day in a restaurant an acquaintance greeted him and asked, 'Hello, André, how are you? How is the watch business?' To which André Heiniger replied, 'I haven't the slightest idea.' His acquaintance laughed, thinking that it was a joke. But André Heiniger retorted, 'No, Rolex is not in the watch business. Rolex is in the luxury, status business.' This affects who are the competitors: not other watch manufacturers but other status symbols, such as gold pens, rings, jewels, mink coats (in the case of ladies' Rolex), being a member of prestigious social clubs and the acquisition of higher priced cars.[1]

The third reason why good definition of mission is important is that if this definition is written in vague terms it is useless and above all a waste of time. In fact most mission statements are a pure waste of time as they consist of vague phrases, full of trivia, such as that they will try to achieve the highest standards of ethical behaviour and professionalism, or that they want to offer products of the highest quality to obtain sufficient profit to repay the shareholders. This type of definition of mission does not show the company's position in the market; it does not define its business and what it wants it to be. Therefore, in recent years, many large and small companies have come face to face with the fact that they do not have a clear definition of their focal point, that is, a clear perception of their mission. As T Levitt says, a vague mission not only does not assemble efforts, but is a loss of prestige as all those outside the institution are aware that it has no clear orientation. It is not necessary to advertise it. If we do not know what we want or where we are going, we should at least keep it to ourselves.

Fourth, even if they are not vague, but explicit (in terms of market position), most mission statements are badly expressed, in that they contain unnecessary elements, but omit necessary ones; and/or they contain elements which are badly considered and thought out. This is highly prejudicial, as a well-defined mission will enable: the formulation of the entrepreneurial *objectives* through which the company will be assessed; a clear definition to be made of the company's *competition*; the selection of the appropriate tactics in *marketing*; and will open the company to market *opportunities*.

Finally the definition of mission contributes towards the concentration of efforts as everyone, from the head of the company down through its workforce, has a common understanding of the essential facts of the business. As performance depends on the focus and the mission statement contributes towards that, it will also contribute towards performance. That is the reason why many conglomerates disperse: at the beginning a sense of mission existed but then it was lost with diversified growth of the company, although spin-offs and recentering were intended to attain a common trunk and capitalize on synergies.

In short there are six reasons for defining a mission well:

1   it defines market options;

2   those options are important;

3   unless made in precise and not vague terms it involves loss of time;

4   and loss of prestige with external agents;

5   mistaken missions have negative results;

6   precise mission statements encourage concentration of effort.

Having established the need to define the mission of an institution well, the way in which to do it is now analysed. As will be seen later on, in order correctly to define the mission (business) of an institution the following must be indicated:

1   the *product/technology* on offer;

2   the *need* served;

3   the type of clients served;

4   the *geographical* area in which the company operates.

These four elements of the mission are the four sides of the strategic square which defines the context of the company, ie its business, its activity (see Figure 6.1).

THE STRATEGIC SQUARE

The idea that the mission of an institution must be seen as a square, defining the context of its market, is the result of a process of evolution. First Levitt, in his classic 1960 article 'Marketing Myopia' (*Harvard Business Review*), called attention to the fact that any definition of mission must include the *need* to be satisfied. This is illustrated by the story which is said to have happened with Peter F Drucker when, at a certain time as a consultant, he visited a company manufacturing glass bottles. The complete board of directors awaited him. Drucker went in, sat down and

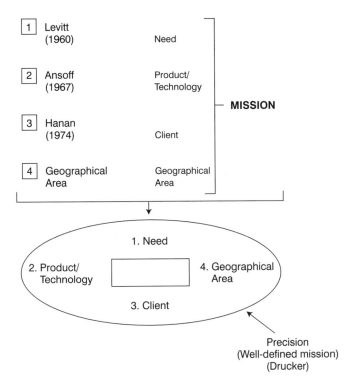

Figure 6.1 The four evolutionary phases in the definition of mission

calmly asked, 'Well, sirs, what is your business?' A heavy silence filled the room. The directors looked at one another, thinking had this famous consultant not done his homework before visiting them to know what was their company's business?

As expected, the chairman of the board of directors cut the uncomfortable silence and said, 'Mr Drucker, our business is to make glass bottles.'

Drucker calmly replied, 'I don't agree. Your business is to make containers. This need can be satisfied by making glass or plastic bottles, cardboard or aluminium cartons or cartons in other metals. For the time being you have opted to satisfy the need for containers exclusively in the form of glass bottles, but you must define your business by the need and not the product and therefore you will keep the opportunities in mind only if you detect both them (the manufacture of other types of containers) and all the choice offered by your competitors (the manufacturers of all possible types of containers).' See Figure 6.2.

In other words, a company's business concerns the need it sets out to satisfy and not the product it uses to satisfy this need. And from the need

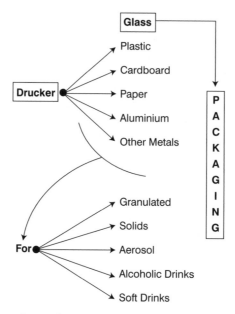

Figure 6.2 Defining the mission by the need

satisfied by the company the opportunities encountered are extracted and the competitors it confronts in the day-to-day market are identified.

Another good example is what happens to cars. Cars can be seen as satisfying different needs: a sense of competence and individualism (Porsche)[2], safety on the road (Volvo), status (Rolls-Royce), economy and easy to drive in cities (Honda Civic), urban and feminine (Nissan Micra), for all types of terrain (Jeep), durable and comfortable driving (BMW, series 3), irreverent, blasé and unconventional (Twingo), robust (Lada), independent (Golf), and liberty, emotion of driving (Renault 19 Cabriolet), etc. Once again, as the need which is to be satisfied changes, so other changes take place in the marketing (message channels), in the competition and in the product characteristics of the product.

Let us look at an example of each of these three aspects. With regard to marketing, let us take the case of Volvo. The manufacturers believe that women are more sensitive to car safety than men. Therefore in spite of the fact that the Volvo is a car driven by men, it is frequently advertised in women's magazines, in the hope that women will influence their husbands to buy this car for safety reasons. Rolls-Royce satisfies the need for status; it does not compete with most of the other cars, but with other status symbols, such as yachts, jewellery, luxury houses, private planes, etc. Finally with reference to the characteristics of the product, the model,

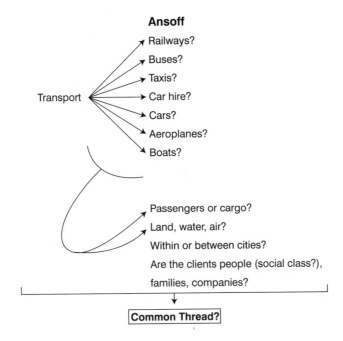

Figure 6.3 The need for indicating the product/technology to define the mission

size, engine capacity, type of coachwork and other characteristics of the car also change in accordance with the need it is intended to satisfy.

Briefly, in accordance with the need it satisfies (company's mission), the opportunities, competitors, marketing and characteristics of the product are different. The mission should be defined by the need (Levitt's argument).

The next step in the evolutionary process of defining mission as a square came in 1965, when Ansoff observed that defining the mission of a company in terms of need is not, generally, enough to provide a useful guide about the company's business.

For example, the transport business can include taxis, hire cars, charter flights, cars, railway and also the construction of boats. They are completely different businesses thus showing that the simple mention of the need does not supply the necessary common thread (see Figure 6.3)

The same applies when considering Scholl, a manufacturer of products for feet, focusing on the need for comfort. First of all, foot comfort can be satisfied by shoes, sandals, powders, lotions or cushioned plasters. In fact Scholl makes these five kinds of products. The marketing – more precisely the distribution channels – differ in accordance with the products manufactured. Some products are distributed through shoe shops (shoes and sandals), other by supermarkets (cushioned plasters) and others in chemists' shops (powders and lotions). In the more general sense, comfort can be satisfied by cars, furniture, interior design, ergonomic chairs, real estate, clothes, etc. It is possible to find makes of all these products which satisfy the need for comfort. But some businesses have absolutely nothing in common with others.

As a result, Ansoff suggested that the mission should indicate the *product* to be offered as well as the need. It is frequently useful to add some information about the technology to be used, as the same product can be based on several alternative technologies. For example, laboratory diagnostic equipment can use: apparatus sensitive to colour, dyes, lasers, pressure, computerized tomography, X-rays or ultrasound. The choice of the technology to be used is critical in terms of its implications.

In a remarkable article published in 1974, 'Reorganize your company around its markets' (*Harvard Business Review*), Hanan introduced a third dimension to the definition of the mission: the definition of the *client*. Hanan argued that including the client dimension in the definition of the business would not just make it more specific, but would create a company which was more responsive to the client's needs.

In fact, as the needs in terms of hardware and software vary according to the client, large companies in the computer sector have frequently opted to have a divisional organization chart per client group, distinguishing between households, professionals, small companies, research centres and medium and large institutions. Within them the computer companies occasionally have specialized divisions in government and public administration, finance, retail, teaching, hotels and industry. For example, Tandy opted to focus its computers on three kinds of clients all having special needs: the professional, the small company and the domestic user. On the other hand, Cray Computers focuses on research centres. Other companies in the industry specialize in other types of clients.

In a similar way, household electrical goods can be sold retail to families or in bulk to private builders.[3] In the former case (retail) the price, delivery date and design are less important whereas service, capacity, durability and the image of the make are more important. In the latter case (private builders) the opposite applies.

It should be mentioned that the importance of defining the client does not just apply to durable goods (computers, electrical appliances), but also to perishable goods or services. As has been mentioned in respect of beers, Michelob specialized in upper-class and Miller in blue-collar drinkers. Coors focuses on the same type of clients as Marlboro (image of virility). Marketing is different according to each type of client.

An example of services is the case of agents/brokers who have traditionally specialized in different types of clients: Paine Webber in women and middle-aged investors with experience; Charles Schweb in specialized workers and investors particularly anxious about the investment's profit (and less concerned with risk); and so on.

Finally, there is a last dimension in the evolution of the square which it is important to include in the definition of the mission: the *geographical dimension*. It is a fact that a change in this dimension can cause an alteration in: the competitors, the characteristics the product must have, the marketing and the opportunities the company encounters.

The geographical dimension has been traditionally used by Japanese companies temporarily to avoid a certain type of competitor and phase the moment in which it will confront them. For example, when Japanese car manufacturers decided to venture into Europe they started by focusing on Finland and Switzerland at the beginning of the 1960s, then at the end of that decade on Benelux (Belgium, The Netherlands and Luxembourg) and Scandinavia. At the beginning of the 1970s they started focusing on Great Britain and only at the end of that decade did they venture strongly into France and Germany.[4] They started their activity and little by little entered into Europe through the countries where the national car industry was nonexistent or weak.

In a similar way, Delta Airlines decided at a particular time to focus on the southeast of the United States to avoid direct competition from Eastern.[5] It then had Dzark, Piedmont and Southern as direct competitors, all companies which had specialized in this geographical area. The *Financial Times* focuses on Europe and the *Wall Street Journal* on North America. Some years ago when the *International Herald Tribune* decided to venture on the British market as a daily newspaper it had to confront new competitors – *The Times* and the *Guardian*. A change in the geographical area of operations does not only imply changes of competitors but also of the necessary characteristics of the product. In fact geography is important whether it be on a national or regional scale.

Let us look at three examples on the national level: the Japanese, American and South American markets. BMW had to change the steering wheel from the right to the left in order to enter the Japanese market. Similarly Boeing had to alter its planes to increase the space for seats and reduce the space for fuel and luggage as most internal journeys in Japan are short. *Mutatis mutandis.* When Toyota decided to enter the American market at the beginning of the 1960s, it studied this market carefully and opted to launch a medium-sized car (Toyota Corona) and no other type of car.

Knorr (manufacturer of instant soup) dominates the market share over Maggi (Nestlé), which is its most direct competitor in some southern European markets – although in blind tests of taste the consumers do not have any preference between the brands – because when Knorr entered these markets, it introduced some kinds of soup adapted to the local customs and preferences. Maggi only adapted later on, but since then has never managed totally to recover the lost ground. Geography represents an important role even on a regional level. This is proved by the success attained by North American companies, such as Lone Star and Vlasic Foods, who adapted the taste of their beer and pickles to the regional markets in which they operate.

Changes in the geographical area also require alterations in *marketing*, both in terms of production as well as distribution channels. Contrary to what happens on the North American market, where one of the critical factors of success for cigarettes is the low level of tar and nicotine, in Latin America the success factors are price and an image associated with economically more developed countries, such as the United States. Hollywood and Manhattan are trade marks for tobacco which try to transmit this type of message, which is then strengthened by appropriate publicity.

Another example is that when the Belgian editor Hergé (of Tintin and Lucky Luke fame) entered the American market, one of the main problems it encountered was access to distribution channels. In Europe, cartoons are usually sold in book shops which often have a specialized section. That does not happen so often in America where the cartoon is usually acquired by newspapers and magazines which publish them in very small excerpts. For this a different style of cartoon is required, where at the end of each small excerpt (usually three or four frames) there is an anecdote or story causing the reader to laugh or smile. That does not happen with Tintin or Lucky Luke as they are different types of cartoons.

Finally the use of the geographical area to define the business draws attention to the opportunities the company encounters: everything which occurs outside the geographical area defined as the centre of operations. If they are opportunities which should be grasped or not is another question, but these opportunities should always be borne in mind. For that to happen, the present geographical area of operations should always be indicated. Thus the American market is an opportunity for the *Financial Times* (which focuses on Europe at the moment); geographical expansion into the whole of the North American market is an opportunity for Coors (which currently focuses on the midwest), and geographical concentration is a possibility for Schlitz which covers all the United States.

As Figure 6.1 shows, the mission/business of an institution must be defined by a square, which we are calling the strategic square, which is the product of an evolution in four phases. Each historical phase contributes one of the sides of the square: the need; the product/technology; the client; and the geographical area.

The advantages of defining the mission with the strategic square are that we shall obtain what Drucker, in his well-known article, 'The Big Power of Little Ideas' argued was precision, in terms of the company 's field of operations – what its business is and is not.

PRECISION AS A VITAL CONDITION FOR DEFINING THE MISSION

By using the four elements of need, product/technology, client and geographical area, both the company's position on the market and the conclusions obtained are exact. For example, the critical factors of success and the type of organization necessary for two manufacturers of air compressors are totally different if one produces portable compressors and the other stationary air compressors, made to the client's specification, of one thousand or more horse power. This ambiguity will be solved if the need and the client are indicated. The former type of compressor is used in road building and civil construction, and the latter in large manufacturing units and in the processing of chemical products.

The same applies to valves which can be mass-produced for taps or nuclear centres and the petrol industry. In this particular case they are made one by one according to the client's specification, or in small series. As a last example, it is not enough to define the mission in terms of air transport. Are we referring to intercontinental, medium or short-haul flights? Transport of passengers or cargo? In the whole of the United States or just in the southeast? And so on[6].

Briefly, by demanding that the definition of the mission includes all four elements (product/technology, need, client and geographical area), the mission is defined in accurate terms. Should one of these elements be missing, the mission statement loses accuracy and, therefore, will be either more difficult to implement or the risk arises of the development of inadequate tactics to implement the company 's strategy.

From the precision of the definition, conclusions referring to four aspects are obtained: the competitors faced; marketing to be developed;

Impact Mission Areas	A Objectives	B Marketing	C Competitors	D Opportunities
1. Need	1	2	3	4
2. Product/Technology	5	6	7	8
3. Client	9	10	11	12
4. Geographical Area	13	14	15	(16)

Total number of
possible modifications

Figure 6.4 Summary of mission areas and impact

the characteristics of the product and the objectives (critical factors of success) to be implemented among the opportunities available (see Figure 6.4). The proof that a mission where one of these four elements is missing is not accurate, and therefore inadequate to be carried out, is given by the fact that if one of the four elements is changed (one of the sides of the strategic square), even if the others remain constant, the conclusions regarding objectives, marketing, competition and opportunities the company has, can be different. This is the theme of the next section.

THE IMPLICATIONS OF DEFINING THE MISSION IN TERMS OF THE STRATEGIC SQUARE

As Figure 6.4 indicates, a change in one or more of the sides of the strategic square (even if the other sides remain constant) can cause changes in objectives, marketing, competitors and opportunities. Let us look at some examples.

Objectives

As was seen previously, there are some critical factors of success that a company has to confront in each market context. The critical factors of success are those tasks or variables (service, publicity, product, research and development, etc) which must be done particularly well to obtain competitive advantage. These success factors are areas where excellence is demanded (contrary to the satisfactory performance needed in all other areas). To be excellent in these areas must therefore be the company 's objective. The areas where special focus and competence are necessary change with the definition of the mission. Sometimes it is enough to change one of the four sides of the master line of the mission for the critical factors of success to change (and therefore the objectives of the company also change).

Scandinavian Airline Systems (SAS) is a good example of this. In the middle of the 1980s when Jan Carlzon became CEO of SAS, he redefined its mission and decided to concentrate on the executive segments of the air transport industry in the whole of Europe, thus, aeroplanes–product; journey–need, executives–clients; Europe–geographical area. The result was that SAS paid less attention to the other areas of the market, such as charters, economy class, cargoes, tourism, low-tariff segment, etc.

By defining its business in this way, SAS acquired its particular success factors. They are: punctuality, safety, individuality and comfort, both on land and in the air. After establishing the objectives (success factors) SAS developed programmes to implement them, which was the same as deciding where the larger part of the company's budget, personnel and management time should go. For example, in order to carry out the objective of providing comfort on land, SAS developed various programmes in which reservations could be made in SAS hotels in several European and American cities. In addition, SAS has a fleet of limousines, helicopters and cars for hire, to transport its passengers from the centre of the city to the airports; in some cities SAS has a special service to take the clients' luggage from their offices or SAS hotels to the airport; special rooms for the passengers were also arranged in the airports with appropriate decoration; the uniform worn by service personnel was altered; the land personnel in the booking offices received extensive training to improve their level of service and ability to deal with exceptional situations, etc. Briefly, their object is to supply door-to-door service.

Marketing

A change in one of the four elements of the master line of the mission can also have implications in terms of marketing tactics to be followed (publicity, message, distribution channels, price, etc). Just two examples presented above will be mentioned for reasons of brevity. In the footwear industry, companies can be found which satisfy fashion needs (C Jourdan), protection against the cold (Sorels), walking on the beach (Jhol), large sizes (Eurico) and comfort (Scholl). As Scholl defined its need as foot comfort, it manufactures shoes with emphasis on comfort and not price, durability, fashion, coolness, etc. Besides shoes it also makes special sandals, cushioned plasters, lotions and powders and its distribution channels are shoe shops, as well as drugstores, supermarkets and chemists.

The decision taken by BMW to launch a quality, higher-priced car – (costing US $40,000–70,000), in addition to its traditional model less than US $40,000) – did not only imply new competitors (from Lincoln, Saab, Volvo, Cadillac and even Mercedes, Jaguar and Cadillac Allendlendé) but also a change in marketing terms. First of all an exhibition room was found in one of the best areas of Park Avenue, in Manhattan; then it started to patronize polo and ski competitions, as well as tennis and squash. Finally, in publicity, the slogans centred on safety, sophistication and luxury.

Competition

It is always important to know the competition – to study its strong and weak points and act accordingly. A precise definition of who are the competitors is only possible if the mission is defined in terms of the strategic square and sometimes it is enough to change one of its sides to lead a company to different conclusions about who are its competitors. One case of this was the way the Japanese car companies entered the European market, as mentioned earlier. Another example is New York Air which, in order to avoid competing directly with United Airlines, changed the client dimension of its mission, from executives to low-price passengers. This meant having recourse to non-union employees, stopping giving meals on board, using low-cost aeroplanes and having very simple and spartan booking offices and rooms in the airports. As well as facilitating the definition of objectives (and programmes), marketing tactics[7] and competition, there is another reason for defining mission in the terms of the strategic square: it makes it easier to detect opportunities and suggest ways for the company to expand its operations with synergy.

Opportunities

By defining its mission with the strategic square, a company can expand its operations in four ways: expansion of products (new products for its operations, keeping all or some of the others as constant sides of the square); expansion of clients (acquire new clients); expansion of needs; and geographical expansion (see Figure 6.5).

Yamaha is a good example of expansion of a product, maintaining the need (leisure), the geographical area (Japan, Europe and the United States) and the type of client (medium/upper class between 20 and 40

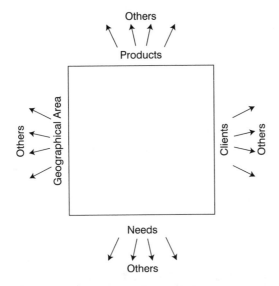

Figure 6.5 The four ways to expand the market

years old). By defining its need as leisure, not transport, Yamaha capitalized on its image, knowledge of the psychology of clients, distribution channels and sales force (to a lesser degree) to commercialize products such as motor cycles, ski equipment, pianos, engines, tennis racquets, etc (see Figure 6.6).[8]

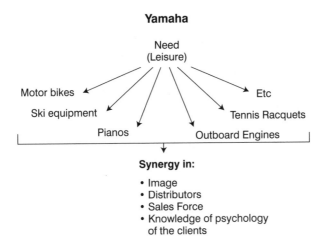

Figure 6.6 Example of Yamaha

At the end of the 1970s, Rockwell International opted to retain as constants the dimensions of the product, the need and the client in its mission statement, and expand its geographical dimension, entering the German and Italian markets with axles and brakes for lorries and cars; Marshall Field expanded its sales operations in the Chicago area to Oregon, Washington, the Carolinas, Ohio and Texas. Some of its competitors opted to expand on other sides of the strategic square, in particular Dayton-Hudson (retail discount shops) and Carlson Pirie Scott (airline catering).

As a last example, Heineken went up from 31st place to the 4th largest in beer companies in just two decades, expanding geographically. Its strategy was to buy regional and local beer companies and keep the makes acquired for itself. As a result today Heineken has 30 makes in the United States, such as Carling, Roinier and Old Style, each one with its regional flavour.

THE FLEXIBILITY OF THE STRATEGIC SQUARE

It is important to note that the use of the strategic square simplifies the discovery of opportunities, as it *makes companies reflect* in precise terms about the characteristics of the market (types of clients, need, etc) that it is seeking to satisfy and, therefore, which clients and needs are put on one side. What is left on one side (outside) are the potential opportunities.

In the United States, the fitted carpet industry is a good example. The industry had been stable until the 1950s and apparently in the long term it would go into irreversible decline. Then the industry carefully analysed who were the main clients at that time and, since then, it has altered the trend of decline. The traditional client of the industry was the housewife and particularly families buying their first house. During that phase the young couple does not have much money for luxuries and therefore puts off the acquisition of carpets. The industry recognized the opportunity to make the builder its client, as covering the floor is one of the few ways of altering the comfort of a house. Therefore the industry reduced the emphasis on sales of carpets to individuals and started to highlight wall-to-wall carpeting, by means of which a cheaply finished floor can be covered, providing a better house at a lower cost for the builder.

In general, companies have the option as to the choice of dimension in which to expand. What frequently happens is that two or more companies faced with the same situation opt for different types of expansion. Gerber and Johnson & Johnson are good examples of this. At the end of the baby-

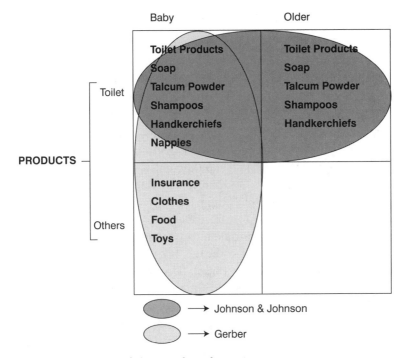

Figure 6.7 Expansion of client and product

boom, Gerber and Johnson & Johnson saw their demand decrease but they opted for different strategies. Gerber opted for an expansion of the product adding baby clothes, life insurance, food and toys to its traditional products, while Johnson & Johnson chose to try to sell their products (toilet products, talcum powder, shampoos and handkerchiefs) to older clients, children under five years of age, young children and youngsters (see Figure 6.7).

As has been shown, the strategic square can operate as a source of opportunities. Now let us look at how it can also generate synergy, associated with these opportunities.

THE STRATEGIC SQUARE AS AN INSTRUMENT FOR SYNERGETIC EXPANSION

When using the strategic square, a company can keep *all* or *some* of the other sides *constant*. *The greater the number of sides changed* the greater the

combination of clients, products, needs and geographical areas and therefore *the greater the number of opportunities.*

On the other hand, *the greater the number of sides remaining constant the
greater is the potential synergy* in the expansion of the market. That is, the
strategic square does not only provide opportunities for expansion of the
companies' operations but also permits expansion with a high synergy
potential to take place.

As seen in Chapter 3, by *positive synergy* we mean the process by which
two divisions, when together in one single institution, are more profitable
than their average if they remain separate entities. That is, two or more
operational units (divisions, companies) working together produce a
larger final result than the sum of the parts.

The importance of synergy is illustrated by the weak result of some
diversification strategies undertaken by tobacco companies. As this
market is mature in developed countries because of the stabilization of
the population, the aging of that population and cultural pressures, the
tobacco companies (British American Tobacco and Rothman International
Imperial Group) opted to diversify in markets which were very attractive
in terms of potential growth and profit (paper, insurance, cosmetics,
wines, medicines, restaurant chains, etc). In practical terms this proved
unsuccessful as, between the *potential* and the *actual* attractiveness of a
new market is the distinctive competence brought to it by a company. The
division of resources (factories, machines, sales force, distribution channels) between its traditional markets and the tobacco market were insufficient and the new markets required a special type of knowledge which
could not be imported from the tobacco market. The management experience and solutions for problems arising in the tobacco market proved to
be inappropriate and inadequate for the new market areas. As a result the
tobacco companies did not have a competitive advantage in these new
markets – their potential attractiveness did not bear fruit in real terms.
There was an abyss between theory and practice.

The advantage of defining a company's mission in terms of the strategic square is exactly to avoid situations of this type as it simplifies the
market expansion with synergy and, therefore, maximizes the possibility
of obtaining competitive advantage over new competitors in new market
areas. A company can decide to expand any one (or more) of the sides of
its strategic square. By keeping the other sides (all or part of them) constant, it will enable the division of resources and transfer of knowledge
and experience between the old and new markets.

When the company decides to keep the *need* side constant, synergy will
occur mainly in the marketing department (sharing of image, distribution

channels, sales force, knowledge of the psychology of the consumer, etc) – see Figure 6.8. The same happens when the dimension of the *client* remains constant, as shown in Figure 6.9. When the *product* is the side of the square which remains constant, the potential for synergy occurs in the production department (knowledge of the workforce, machines, warehouses, etc). Beneteau, in Figure 6.10, is an example. Finally, when the geographical area is kept constant, as is the case of Penn Central in Figure 6.11, the potential for synergy exists in the personnel departments (same salary scales, same labour law, similar career plans, etc) and/or financial and accounting departments (internal financing between units, shared contacts with the financial institutions, management control system and analytic accounting, etc).

Briefly, depending on the side of the square (mission dimension) which was altered and those which remain constant, the synergy will mainly

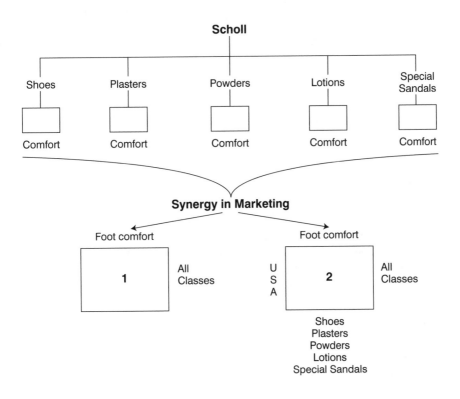

Figure 6.8 Synergy and Scholl

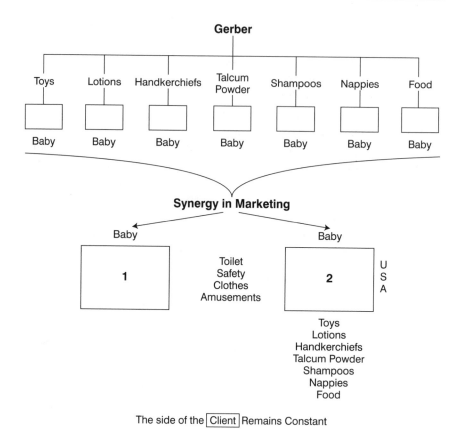

Figure 6.9 Synergy and Gerber

occur in one or another functional department (production, marketing, personnel and finance - see Figure 6.12). The level of synergy obtained in a given market expansion procedure depends on the number of sides (dimensions) which remain constant. A maximum synergy potential occurs when just one side is changed and all the others remain constant. For example, when the Swiss watch manufacturers decided to include the manufacture of precision instruments for aeroplanes in their range they obtained high levels of synergy as the product, the need and the geographical area all remained constant and only the client was new.

Similarly, some years ago when the cosmetic and skin treatment companies launched a specific range for men, their synergy derived from continuing with the same type of product, need and geographical area (as only the client was changed). Finally, in the 1980s the strategic movement of the Japanese banks to follow Japanese industries to the US market benefited. The product, the need and the client remained constant (the focal

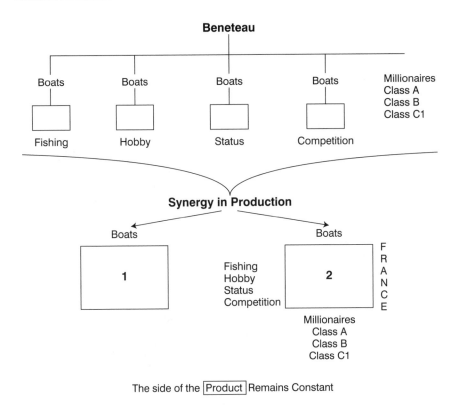

Figure 6.10 Synergy and Beneteau

point of Japanese banks is mainly Japanese companies operating in the market in the United States) and only the geographical area changed (from Japan to the United States).

The greater the number of sides remaining constant between the various strategic squares (business areas) in which the company is engaged, the greater the level of synergy. For example, if a company has 10 business units (strategic business units – SBUs) it will have 10 strategic squares or business areas.[9] All 10 can be completely different on all four sides, or just three, or just two, or just one. When all the 10 squares are different on all four sides, the company is a conglomerate and there is no synergy between any of its business units. The more common sides there are between all the squares, the greater the synergy will be.

So an indicator of the synergy level in a company[10] is:

$$\frac{\text{number of common sides} \times \text{number of strategic squares in which it occurs}}{4 \times \text{total number of strategic squares in which the company operates}}$$

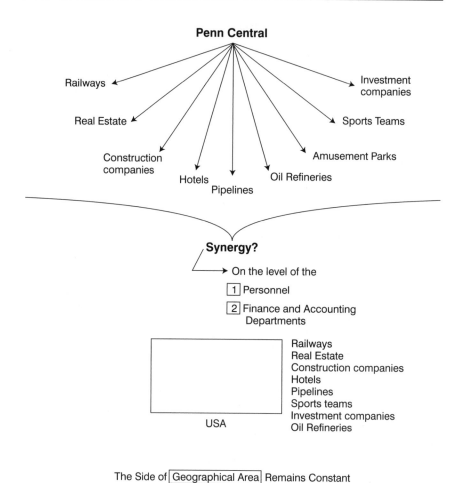

Figure 6.11 Synergy and Penn Central

It should be noted that *the bigger the fraction the greater the synergy within the company.* It varies between 0 (when the number of common sides is 0) and 3/4 (when there are three common sides among all the squares). Intermediary situations can and frequently do occur. For example, if five squares have three common sides and another five have two, we have:

$5 \times 3 = 15$
$5 \times 2 = 10$
$15 + 10 = 25$
$25/40 = 5/8 = 62.5\%$

Common side / Synergy Dept.	Product	Need	Client	Geographical Area
Production	✓			
Marketing		✓	✓	
Personnel				✓
Accounting				✓
Finance				✓

Figure 6.12 The strategic square and synergy

In this situation the synergy is stronger than if, for example, four squares had three common sides, four had two common sides and two were completely different from all the others. In this case we would have:

$4 \times 3 = 12$
$4 \times 2 = 8$
$2 \times 0 = 0$
$12 + 8 + 0 = 20$
$20/40 = 1/2 = 50\%$

Briefly, the value of the top ratio, which varies between 0 and 3/4, is an indicator of the potential level of synergy existing between the various markets in which the company operates (its strategic squares) and it varies in ordinal terms. Similarly, the measure of diversity (see Chapter 4) was another ordinal indicator of synergy. For cardinal terms, the indicator of synergy presented in Chapter 3 should be used.

THE MISSION STATEMENT AS A SYNTHESIS OF STRATEGY

When defining a mission – the business of an institution – a distinction must be made between whether it is the mission of a strategic business unit or the company as a whole. If it is a division of a company then its mission/business must be defined indicating the four sides of the strategic square: product; client; need; and geographical area. Thus, for example, the mission of the first of the Scholl divisions in Figure 6.8 is the manufacture of shoes with emphasis on comfort for all social classes in the United States. In the same way, the definition of the first division of Gerber in Figure 6.9 is the manufacture of toys for the entertainment of babies in the whole world. That is, the definition of the business on the divisional level must include these four elements: product, client, need and geographical area.

Figure 6.13 presents some other examples of definitions of mission on the divisional level. On the corporate level, the mission is defined either by indicating all the products, all the clients, all the needs and geographical areas in which the company operates or preferably indicating what is common in all the divisions (strategic squares) of the company – see Figure 6.14. Therefore, taking the examples in Figures 6.8 to 6.10, Scholl's mission is 'foot comfort in the United States', Gerber's is 'babies are our business' and Beneteau's is 'we make boats in France'. According to Figure 6.6, Yamaha will define its business as 'leisure' and Johnson & Johnson as 'toilet products'– see Figures 6.7 and 6.9.

The mission statement for the corporate level expresses what is common between the squares devoted to its various divisions. If the

Timex
Low priced watches for *lower social classes* in the *United States*

Holiday Inn
Motels for *travellers* of social classes B and C *to stay overnight* in the *United States*

Rolex
Watches which are jewellery items and *status* symbols for the *upper class* (A+) *the whole world over*

Cunard Steamship
Boats acting as hotels and *floating recreational* resorts for the *middle class* in the *United States*

Beneteau
Boats for *professional fishermen* in *France*

Note:	
	Product
	Need
	Client
	Geographical Area

Figure 6.13 Divisional definitions of mission

Scholl
Foot *comfort* in the *United States*

Beneteau
Boats in *France*

Gerber
Babies are our business

Yamaha
Leisure is our business

Note:
Product
Need
Client
Geographical Area

Johnson & Johnson
Toilet products

Figure 6.14 Corporate definitions of mission

product is common, the product is used to define the mission. If it is the client, the client is used. If it is the need, that is used. If it is more than one of these, then all the common elements are used. If there is no common element, there is not one mission for the company as a whole, but various sub-missions (for various areas of the company). A company which does not have a mission but has several sub-missions is usually called a *conglomerate*. Also there will be no synergy between sub-missions, but in the optimum cases there will be a limited amount of synergy between some of the company's divisions. This shows why the present tendency for spin-offs, sticking to core competence, recentering, etc (equivalent terms) occurs.

FIFTEEN QUESTIONS ABOUT THE DEFINITION OF MISSION

At this point it would perhaps be useful to systemize some of the basic principles of definition of mission and its relationship with other concepts, such as objectives, strategy and philosophical guides. Table 6.1 presents 15 questions which will be replied to very concisely afterwards with the fundamental objective of organizing ideas.[11]

Let us start at the beginning. The advantage of defining the mission was presented in the introduction to this chapter. The fundamental reason is that by defining the mission and transmitting it to all the company staff a contribution is made towards the concentration of efforts and therefore performance. That is:

mission -> focus -> performance

Table 6.1 Questions about the definition of mission

1. What is the advantage of defining the mission?

2. Why include the four elements – product, client, need and geographical area – in the definition of mission?

3. What is the use of defining the mission in terms of the strategic square?

4. Why not include other elements in the mission?

5. Why is there no determinism in the management of the strategic square?

6. What is the relationship between each SBU and the strategic square?

7. What is the relationship of the mission on the business level and the corporate level?

8. What is the relationship between the mission on the corporate level and synergy?

9. What is the relationship between strategy and mission?

10. What is the relationship between segment and the strategic square?

11. What is the relationship between the strategic square and the strategy typologies?

12. Is the geographical area really necessary? And the global markets?

13. What is the relationship between philosophical guides and mission?

14. What is the relationship between mission and objective?

15. What publicity should be given to the notion of mission?

Second, why include the four elements in the definition of mission? Only in that way will the business, the area where the company operates, be unmistakably defined, observing the precision and detail which Peter F Drucker argued should be used to define a company's business.[12] This is illustrated in Figure 6.15 by Ansoff's classical example referring to transport.

Third, what is the advantage of defining the mission by the strategic square? The advantage is that from the function of product, client, need and geographical area come objectives, marketing, competitors and opportunities. If one of the former group is changed, then one of latter may also change. This is illustrated in Figure 6.16, where examples given

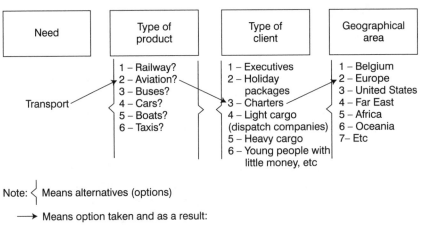

Need	Type of product	Type of client	Geographical area
	1 – Railway?	1 – Executives	1 – Belgium
	2 – Aviation?	2 – Holiday packages	2 – Europe
	3 – Buses?		3 – United States
Transport	4 – Cars?	3 – Charters	4 – Far East
	5 – Boats?	4 – Light cargo (dispatch companies)	5 – Africa
	6 – Taxis?	5 – Heavy cargo	6 – Oceania
		6 – Young people with little money, etc	7– Etc

Note: Means alternatives (options)

→ Means option taken and as a result:

1 – the competitors
2 – the objectives (types of planes, timetable, personnel training, etc)
3 – marketing
4 – opportunities
are different

Figure 6.15 The mission defined in a specific way

Alterations in the mission areas \ Implications	A Objectives	B Marketing	C Competitors	D Opportunities
1. Needs	– Compressors – Footwear	– Footwear – BMW – Kleenex	– Packaging – Rolex – Cunard Steamship	– Packaging – Yamaha – Scholl
2. Product/Technology	– Transport – Laboratory Equipment	– Scholl	– Beneteau – Timex	– Beneteau – Gerber
3. Cslient	– Computers – Electric household appliances – Valves – SAS – Carpets	– Computers – Electric household appliances – Beers	– New York Air – Holiday Inn	– Brokers – Restaurants – Johnson & Johnson – Holiday Inn
4. Geographical Area	– BMW – Boeing – Toyota – Classic Foods – Hergé	– Lonestar – South America Cigarettes – Hergé – Coffee	– Japanese car companies – Delta Airlines – Boeing	– Newspapers – Rockwell – Heineken – Penn Central – Coffee

Figure 6.16 Examples

during this chapter have been put into into the various cells used in Figure 6.4.

When the operational area of a company is defined in terms of the strategic square(s), not only are the four areas of possible expansion indicated (modification of the product and/or client and/or need and/or geographical area), but also whether these areas of expansion will be synergetic if one or more of the other three sides remain constant. That means the instrument of the strategic square offers the strategist a great degree of flexibility.

Which side(s) of the strategic square to expand is usually a decision to be taken by the company – an option which must be evaluated according to: the number of existing alternatives, the level of synergy for each one, the level of competition, the size of the market and the company's strong points. A good example of this flexibility is given in Figure 6.7 above, which shows how Gerber and Johnson & Johnson expanded synergetically but in different directions. They initially had the same mission derived from the same client (babies), need (hygiene) and products (talcum powder, shampoos, handkerchiefs and nappies). Johnson & Johnson retained the need as a constant and expanded to older clients (as well as babies, children up to five years old, juveniles and youngsters) through various toilet products (shampoos, deodorants, soap, etc). Gerber retained the client (babies) as a constant and decided to expand by serving other needs and therefore launched clothes, various kinds of food, toys and even life insurance in favour of the new-born. This example proves that the strategic square is a powerful instrument first of all to generate and then to select between various strategic options.

Fourth, why not include other elements in the mission? For two reasons.[13] First of all phrases like 'We want to maximize the profit or to give the shareholders good profit' are platitudes similar to a person saying they want to be happy. The real question lies in what the person is going to do about it. What is the business/mission in which the company will be present? Then the mission statement is intended to summarize, to capture the essence of the position of the company on the market. Immediately, less is more.

Fifth, why is there no determinism in the management of the strategic square? Because at times it is possible to change one side without altering the others. Several examples have been given in this chapter – in the areas of air transport (SAS), electric household appliances, carpets, computers, Johnson & Johnson, etc (see Figure 6.16) – of the change of the side of the client while the others remained constant. Examples have been given of the change of the side of need, as in the case of Rolex, footwear and several makes of cars, like the VW Beetle, Porsche, Rolls-Royce, Alfa Romeo Spider, Honda Civic, Volvo 360, Nissan Micra and BMW.

When considering change to the side of product/technology while maintaining the other sides constant, examples of laboratory equipment, Timex, transport, etc were analysed. Most of the cases covered in this chapter can be considered as examples of changes in the geographical area, as most of them involved alterations in the region in which they work occurred (BMW, Toyota, Hergé, *Financial Times*, Penn Central, etc) – see Figure 6.16. In any case it is important to remember that by changing one side, even if the others remain constant, the objectives, marketing, competitors and/or opportunities can be seen distinctly, as summarized in Figure 6.16.

Sixth, what is the relationship between each strategic business unit and the strategic square? The relationship must be one to one. That is, there must be as many SBUs[14] as strategic squares, as each one is a definite market. Of course between the top of the company and the manager of an SBU there can and must be intermediate hierarchical degrees of coordination. The more there are the greater the number of strategic squares and SBUs.

Seventh, what is the relationship of the mission on the business level and the corporate level? On the business level, the mission must be defined by the four elements of each square: product, client, need, geographical area. On the corporate level, the mission must be defined solely using the common element(s) of the various squares. In either case, the company as a whole does not have one mission but several sub-missions. It is a conglomerate.

Eighth, what is the relationship between the mission on the corporate level and synergy? Basically there is only synergy on the global level of the institution (between all its SBUs) if it is possible to define one mission at the corporate level. If there is more than one mission at the corporate level (for several groups of SBUs), then there will be as many synergy zones as sub-missions.[15]

Ninth, what is the relationship between strategy and mission? As shown in Chapters 2 and 3, strategy concerns where the institution is; that is, its position in the market. A mission statement is a phrase (the simplest and shortest possible) which captures the essence of this position in the market. The mission statement defines and synthesizes the strategy. Therefore the mission can only be defined after the strategy has been chosen (geographic areas, industries and segments).

Tenth, what is the relationship between segment and strategic square? As mentioned in Chapter 2, a segment is a sub-group of clients which has specific needs in the purchase of a product. That is, there are three of the four elements of the mission (sides of the strategic square) in the definition of a segment, all except the geographical area. Therefore the relationship between segment and strategic square is direct and refers to the side of the geographical area. Either the geographical area is sufficiently large to cover the whole segment or it intersects the segment. In the former case, the segment is equal to the strategic square. In the latter case, it is larger. Thus the strategic square is smaller than or equivalent to a segment.

Let us look at a hypothetical example: coffee for expresso machines for class A homes in the Midwest and Southeast of the United States. Either the criteria for the purchase by this type of clients in this geographical area are different from those for the same type of clients in the rest of the country – and thus the strategic square defined above coincides with the segment – or the criteria for purchase are the same, and then the strategic square is a sub-group of a segment. Then why indicate the geographical area? Because, as seen above, it delineates the competitors, focuses the marketing (promotion and distribution channels), establishes the objectives (critical factors of success) and calls attention to the existing opportunities for geographical expansion.

Eleventh, what is the relationship between the strategic square and the typologies of strategy? A typical typology differentiates between the seven types of strategies shown below:

1   growth within the present area of strategic business: increase of the market share, increase in the use of the product through greater quantity and/or frequency;

2   new applications for present clients;

3   new geographical area;

4   new products;

5   new clients;

6   unrelated diversification;

7   vertical integration: upstream and downstream.

It is easy to see that strategy 1 corresponds to accentuating the venture in the present strategic square and strategies 2, 3, 4 and 5 correspond to the alteration of one of the sides of the strategic square (keeping or not keeping the others). Strategy 6 corresponds to entry in a totally different strategic square. Therefore the strategic square allows consideration of all the

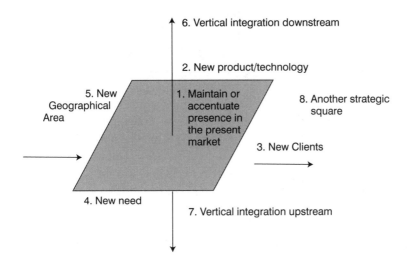

Figure 6.17 The strategic square and the eight types of possible strategies

alternative strategies with the exception of vertical integration. When using it as an instrument to outline the strategy it must always be remembered that it refers to a certain stage of production. With this in mind the strategic square synthesizes and covers all the possible alternatives. In order to consider strategic alternatives which include various stages of production a document like the one in Figure 6.17 can be used and serves as a reminder.

Twelfth, is the geographical area really necessary? And the global markets? Global markets refer to the existence of the same type of clients with identical needs available to acquire a product regardless of the geographical area. That is, it is possible to find the same segment (clients with identical needs) in several countries throughout the world. This is the meaning of the concept of global markets. If this is so, why use the geographical dimension to delineate this area of the institution's activity? For three reasons. First of all, despite the tendency for homogeneity there are still cultural particularities in the various geographic zones, which have implications for the objectives and marketing within these zones, as shown in the examples in cells 13 and 14 in Figure 6.16 and developed earlier in this chapter. Even if that does not happen or happens to a very small degree and tends to occur less and less often, by using the geographical dimension both the competitors are being managed (some chosen and others avoided) and attention is being called to the possibilities of geographical expansion which could otherwise remain unnoticed.

Briefly, the geographical area should be used to define the mission as the global markets do not exist 100 per cent for all products and because, even if there is a global market for the product (model) in question, the determination of the geographical area allows attention to be paid to the concentration of marketing efforts, allows management of the competitors and emphasizes the opportunities for geographical expansion.

Thirteenth, what is the relationship between philosophical guides and mission? Besides mission, business literature also talks about philosophical guides. These philosophical guides are used by companies in their internal magazines, for clients, in their reports and accounts, when institutional advertisements are published, and on placards in their auditoriums, canteens and conference rooms. They include sentences such as:

> *May Kay Cosmetics: A spirit of sharing and looking after others when time is given with pleasure, understanding and experience.*
>
> *Dow Chemical: To share the obligation of protecting the environment.*
>
> *Pfizer: To contribute towards social well-being and act as a good citizen on a local and national level in all the countries in which we work.*
>
> *Crown Cork: A company does not exist just for the well-being of a group, whether they be consumers, shareholders, companies or public, but for the well-being of everyone together.*
>
> *General Electric: Progress is our most important product.*
>
> *Union Carbide: The company of discoveries.*
>
> *IBM: The best service company in the world.*
>
> *Pepsi Cola: Our business is marketing.*
>
> *RCA: The name of greatest confidence in electronics.*

Regarding these sentences, it should be noted that they are not definitions of mission. Phrases such as those of May Kay Cosmetics, Dow Chemical or Pfizer do not say anything about the company's business. They do not define what they do to earn their living. Computers? Plastics? Textiles? In the United States? In Denmark? For clients of the chemical industry? For small companies? For other clients? etc. Nothing of this is emphasized in the above definitions.

So what is the purpose of these expressions? When they are used as mentioned above in company magazines, placards, accounts, institutional advertisements, etc, these expressions fulfil two objectives: first, they transmit a certain image to the outside world and, second, they create a certain culture of the company. Thus philosophical guides are instruments for the creation of an image such as publicity, public relations and other marketing areas and creation of a certain entrepreneurial culture, involving such things as the incentives system operating in the company, the company's decoration and environment, the procedures manual and the dress code. Image and culture are the objectives of philosophical guides. They should not be confused with the definition of mission which, as was seen earlier on, captures and defines the essence of the company's strategy.

A last aspect to be mentioned is that both the philosophical guides and the mission can be defined only after the company has chosen its strategy (geographical areas, industries and segments). Only after this decision has been made can it be synthesized in a phrase (mission statement) and then decisions can be taken regarding the image which should be transmitted and the culture to be created.

Fourteenth, what is the relationship between mission and objectives? On the business level, the mission statement is a phrase which contains the four sides of the strategic square. Each strategic business unit (SBU) must concentrate on a strategic square which is its market. In order for a company to be successful in this market it must meet certain objectives, among which are the critical factors of success of this market, attaining a certain level of annual profitability (determined by hierarchical superiors), and market share. That is, the objectives are areas within the strategic square in which the SBU is concentrating and where it must obtain excellence. The mission is the four sides of the square contained in a phrase - see Figure 6.18.[16]

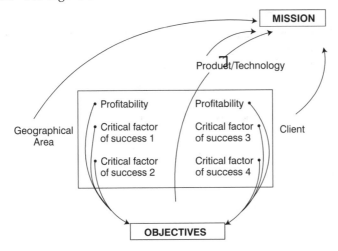

Figure 6.18 The relationship between mission and objectives

And last but not least, what publicity should be given to the company's mission? If it is considered that the mission statement is the synthesis of the strategy, this question is the equivalent of asking what publicity a company should give to its strategy. Obviously every company should be aware of its competitors, and conceal its strategy from them. But in order to provide a spirit of unity and concentration of effort, the company's employees might need to know the strategy. However, if it is publicized to all of them there is the risk that the information will leak outside.

So a distinction must be made between the mission at the business level (which goes into detail) and the corporate mission which can be one of two kinds: either detailed indicating all the products, clients, etc (see Figure 6.8), or just a general outline presenting what is common between all the businesses. An acceptable compromise solution seems to be to inform only the top staff of the institution of the mission on a corporate detailed level. The corporate general mission can (and must) be widely publicized. In any case it must be periodically re-evaluated as is the case with the strategy. Mission statements must also be periodically rewritten when strategy is altered.

CONCLUSION

This chapter illustrated that the business of an institution – its mission – must be defined using four elements: its product/technology, the need satisfied, the basis of its clientele and the geographical area of operations. These four elements are the four sides of the strategic square which define the borders of the company's business and comprise the product of a historical evolution referring to the concept of how to define the mission.

Changing one of these sides can imply a change in one or more of the four elements: objectives, marketing, competition and opportunities. This last aspect is worth emphasizing, as it suggests ways of expanding the company's operations with a high level of synergy. Synergy exists provided that at least one of the sides of the strategic square remains constant. The greater the number of sides remaining constant, the greater the level of synergy. This is particularly important as it is easier for companies to diversify successfully if they maintain a common nucleus (core) for all their operations. As Archimedes the scientist said, 'Give me somewhere to stand, and I will move the earth.'

7

Strategic reorientation

Napoleon Bonaparte

INTRODUCTION

This chapter will present a *dynamic* measure of strategy since all measures covered in the earlier chapters were static. Indeed, previous chapters defined the strategy (through the strategic plan – Chapter 3); quantified it (Chapter 4); qualified it (Chapter 5); and synthesized it (Chapter 6). However, quantification (in terms of four variables), qualification (in terms of the four large categories) and definition of the mission (business in which the company is engaged) all refer to the current strategy: where the company is and where it presently invoices; its clients, its industries, its geographical areas.

Nothing guarantees that the current strategy is the ideal one. Therefore strategic plans are made periodically indicating the segments (types of clients), the industries and the geographical areas in which the company will venture. Consequently there may be smaller or greater differences between the current strategy and the new strategy which is intended to be implemented (shown by the strategic plan). They can be absolutely the same and, in that case, the strategic plan indicates a strategy of continuity. Or they can be completely different if the industrial, geographical area and segment recommended by the strategic plan are 100 per cent different from the current ones.

Between one extreme situation and the other, there are degrees of intermediate *strategic reorientation* and therefore it is interesting to be able to assess the level of reorientation imposed on the company by the strategic plan. That is the aim of this chapter: to present three ways in which the concept of strategic reorientation can be assessed.

> *It is a bad plan that cannot be corrected.*
>
> NAPOLEON BONAPARTE
>
> *Plans are nothing; what counts is the planning.*
>
> DWIGHT E EISENHOWER

The concept and its evaluation have three basic advantages. First, the concept allows a company to assess whether it has adapted for better or worse to its present fit in the environment. The greater the strategic reorientation, the less adapted is the company's present position on the market; that is, its *efficiency* is less.[2] Second, the amount of strategic reorientation the company intends to make will also influence the level of necessary organizational alterations; that is, the degree of *internal readjustment necessary to obtain efficiency*. Thus, by evaluating how much the company needs to change, inferences can be drawn about its level of efficiency and conclusions can be reached regarding the amount of alteration that is necessary. When very great reorganization is implied by strategic reorientation, before starting it is useful to re-examine all the strategic plan's suppositions and conclusions to ensure there are no mistakes. This is the third advantage of evaluating the concept of strategic reorientation.

	A Industries	B Segments
I Present Strategy (where the company invoices, sells at the moment)	A	B
II Future Strategy (based on the company's new strategic plan)	C	D
Difference between I and II (B(A) – D(C))	Degree of Strategic Reorientation	

To simplify things it is assumed that the geographical area is constant

Figure 7.1 Present and future strategy

THE CONCEPT OF STRATEGIC REORIENTATION

Within the concept of strategy it is possible to differentiate between two basic types: the present strategy and the future strategy proposed for the company (see Figure 7.1). The present strategy is that which, supposedly, is the result of the implementation of the previously prepared strategic plan or, if that plan does not exist, from the simple daily evolution of the institution. It is the combination of segments (of the industries) where the company invoices (sells). The present strategy is not a matter of opinion or debate, but a simple confirmation of fact, which is verified by the list of clients (whether computerized or not) or, when it does not exist, from a sample of who was invoiced (and how much) in the last three, four or six months.

In contrast, the future strategy is not a matter of fact but of intentions, as it refers to the segments of the industries where the company intends to venture in the future. This group of intentions is summarized in a document which is the new strategic plan: the strategic plan which has just been finished (or is almost finished).

Thus, there can be *total, partial or no agreement* (ie total divergence) between the strategic plan which has just been prepared and the present strategy. The first happens when the strategic plan indicates the preservation of the same segments (in the same industries), without abandoning any of them and without embarking into new segments, and the invoicing percentage in each of them (referring to the total of the company) will also be supposedly maintained. Here the strategic reorientation is non-existent.

Strategic reorientation is total when the new strategic plan advises that a venture should be made into *totally different* segments from the previous ones, which will mean abandoning the present segments, and that the company's invoicing (sales) will be from completely new areas. In most cases, the new strategic plan will indicate an *intermediate* situation between the two above situations – that is, a partial strategic reorientation – either because the company intends to alter the invoicing in some of the present segments, referring to the total sales of the company, and/or because some of the old segments have been abandoned; and/or because new segments have been entered.

In any of these cases, it is interesting to develop a measurement of the amount of reorientation of the company contemplated in the strategic plan. This repositioning on the market[3] can vary between zero and 100 per cent, just as pilots in a plane or drivers of a car can decide to keep on track or make a turn of X degrees according to what is appropriate in terms of the route.

Three ways will now be presented by which the degree of reorientation implied by the strategic plan can be calculated.[4] The first method is the simplest, and the least accurate. In the second method the strategic plan indicates two kinds of segments which we shall call stars and blacks; that is, segments in which the company will or will not venture. In the third method the strategic plan also differentiates a third type of segment – those types of clients which will not be actively sought but which if they contact the company will be supplied (passive attitude – neutral segments). This is in contrast to the star segments, which consist of clients actively sought after (focus of the active commercial activity and the marketing budget), and blacks which it has been deliberately decided not to supply.

THE SIMPLEST METHOD OF CALCULATING STRATEGIC REORIENTATION

The simplest way of calculating the strategic reorientation is:

1   list the segments which the company occupies at the moment;

2   list the segments in which it will venture (according to the strategic plan);

3 establish the number of different segments between 1 and 2;

4 divide this number by the total segments in 1 or 2, whichever is the larger.

In order to simplify this, the names of industries and segments will be dispensed with. For example, suppose that a company is in two industries: 1 and 2. In industry 1 it occupies segments A, B and D, and in industry 2 segments C, E and F. Thus the present strategy consists of segments: A1, B1, D1, C2, E2 and F2. Suppose the company, according to its strategic plan, intends to remain in all these segments except B1, which it will abandon, and will enter segment H of industry 2 and L of industry 3. Therefore the new strategy according to the plan is: A1 (which remains); B1 (*abandoned*); D1 (which remains); C2 (which remains); E2 (which remains); F2 (which remains); H2 (*new segment* of the old industry); L3 (*new segment,* new industry). The degree of strategic reorientation is 3/7; multiplying by 100 per cent, equals 43 per cent (three segments corresponding to one abandoned and two new ones; seven referring to the present position).

If there is another new segment (eg R3), or if another old segment is abandoned (eg A1), a degree of strategic reorientation would be obtained of 4/8 (50 per cent) and 4/6 (66 per cent) respectively. This illustrates one of the three drawbacks of this calculation. The first drawback is that it is more sensitive to the abandonment of segments than to the entry into new ones, as in the former case the denominator does not increase, while in the latter it increases. Second, it does not take into account that the objectives of invoicing in each segment need not remain constant. Third, it only works with two types of segments (where the company is and is not), and does not take into account a third possible type of segment: those which the company is in but which it considers as secondary.

The next calculation of strategic reorientation corrects the first two drawbacks. The third calculation to be presented will also preclude the third drawback. As the calculation methods presented later are more sophisticated, an actual market segmentation matrix is used to illustrate and qualify the presentation of the analysis.

THE SECOND METHOD OF CALCULATING STRATEGIC REORIENTATION

A second calculation of the degree of strategic reorientation can be obtained by using four steps:

1   The company segments its market using the most appropriate dimensions (product, client, need and/or geographical area). The choice depends on the characteristics of the industry. The output is a matrix such as that shown in Figure 7.2, which represents possible segmentation of the engineering services market. In this example, the two dimensions used are the products (services) and the type of clients.

2   The segmentation matrix must have three kinds of cells: shadowed cells representing empty or almost uninhabited segments; white cells representing segments where the company could be situated, but where it is not (does not invoice at the present time); and cells containing numbers indicating the company's invoicing percentage in those segments. The totals are added up in lines or columns, totalling of course 100 per cent (in the lower right-hand corner). The company's present strategy is the group of segments where it invoices.

3   Now let us imagine that company A developed a new strategic plan with new segments into which it decides to venture. For each of these segments the company has certain expectations for invoicing in the next year or two. In some companies these expectations are realized in terms of objectives of sales volume; in others in terms of the market share. However, as Karl von Clausewitz, one of the great interpreters of Napoleon, said, 'Strategy is where you are and with what strength.' Therefore it is important that the invoicing expectations (objectives) of all the segments are brought together to obtain the relative weight of each segment (what it will represent in terms of the total invoicing percentage of the company).

4   Now the difference between 2 and 3 is calculated in terms of the formula:

$$\frac{\sum |\text{Segment x} - \text{J Segment x}|}{200} \times 100$$

$$x = 1, 2, 3, \text{etc. n}$$

		A	B	C	D	E	F	G	
					Private				
	Type of Services	Central Admin.	Regional Admin.	Local Authority	Industry	Real Estate	State Owned Enterprises	Cooperatives	Total
1	Special Infrastructure (Large Systems)	20		10					30
2	Ordinary Infrastructure								
3	Water Supply Treatment				10				10
4	Sewage Treatment			30					30
5	AA. Planning Syst								
6	Drainage Planning Syst								
7	Solid Residue Plan								
8	Solid Residue Spec. Works								
9	Solid Residue Ord. Works								
10	Hydraulic Works/Dams								
11	Hydraulic Works/Irrigation		25						25
12	Hydraulic Works Floods/Regul./Rivers		5						5
13	Environmental/Pollution								
14	Project Management								
15	Training								
16	Fiscalization								
17	Assessment/Audit								
18	Civil Eng. — Spec. Struc (1)								
19	Civil Eng. — Buildings (2)								
20	Civil Eng. — Com. Roads (3)								
21	Territorial Planning								
22	Energy (4)								
23	Prod Systems engineering								
	Total	20	30	40	10				100

(1) Bridges; Viaducts; Works of Art, etc (2) Hotels; Large Buildings, etc (3) Roads Traffic, etc (4) Geotechnical; atomic, etc

Figure 7.2 The segmentation matrix of an engineering services company

in which

> F Segment x = Percentage that invoicing in segment x represents at
> present in the total invoicing of the company

> J Segment x = Percentage that invoicing in segment x represents in the
> strategic plan referring to the total of the company

and three situations can occur:

A. Strategic maintenance

The invoicing envisaged in the strategic plan corresponds entirely to the present situation. In this case the value of the ratio is 0 per cent (as its numerator is nil) and the degree of strategic reorientation is *nil*.

B. Total strategic alteration

The company will abandon all the present segments and venture into new segments. The value of the ratio is *100 per cent* (as the numerator is 200).

C. Partial strategic alteration

Two situations can occur:

C1 The company remains in exactly the same segments, but with different invoicing percentages.

C2 The company not only alters the invoicing percentages in its present segments, but also abandons some of them and/or ventures into new ones.

In both in C1 and the C2 situations, the ratio varies between 0 and 100 per cent. The nearer it is to 100 per cent, the greater the significance of:

1 the alterations in the invoicing in the present segments;

2 the segments abandoned in the previous invoicing;

3 the new segments in the present invoicing.

Figure 7.3 presents the value of the ratio for the various possible situations in which the strategic plan differs from the present reality (or the new plan differs from the previous plan). It should be noted that the more factors mentioned in the above paragraph are present, the greater will be the value of the ratio of strategic reorientation, which will increase from the scenario with the least alteration (Hypothesis I) to the scenario with the greatest alteration (Hypothesis IV).

A MORE DETAILED CONCEPT OF STRATEGIC REORIENTATION

Another possibility in terms of the strategic plan is not only to differentiate between star and black segments but also to introduce a new category: the neutral segments. It is understood that *star segments* are those in which the company has competitive advantage and/or are very attractive in terms of sales volume and growth. The *neutral segments* are average

Present strategy

Cell   1A - 20%
Fig 7.2 1C - 10%
     3D - 10%
     4C- 30%
    11B - 25%
    12B - 5%

New strategy

Hypothesis I	Hypothesis II	Hypothesis III	Hypothesis IV
Cell 1A - 15%	Cell 1A - 5%	Cell 1A - 0%	Cell 1A - 0%
1C - 15%	1C - 30%	1C - 30%	1C - 30%
3D - 10%	3D - 10%	3D - 10%	3D - 0%
4C- 40%	4C- 45%	4C- 45%	4C- 45%
11B - 20%	11B - 0%	11B - 0%	11B - 0%
12B - 10%	12B - 10%	12B - 15%	12B - 0%
			13B - 10%
			13C - 15%

Value of the ratio: Value of the ratio: Value of the ratio:

$$\frac{5+5+0+10+5+5}{200} \times 100 = $$

$$= 15\%$$

$$\frac{15+20+0+15+25+5}{200} \times 100 = $$

$$= 40\%$$

$$\frac{20+20+0+15+25+10}{200} \times 100 = \frac{=90}{200}$$

$$= 45\%$$

Value of the ratio:

$$\frac{20+20+10+15+25+5+10+15}{200} \times 100 = $$

$$= 60\%$$

Figure 7.3 Simulation of the value of the strategic reorientation ratio (2nd calculation formula)

Commercial Activity Active		Focus on the commercial budget	Acceptance of request for orders appearing passively
Star Segments	A Yes	D Yes	G Yes
Neutral Segments	B No	E Yes	H Yes
Black Segments	C No	F No	I No

Notes:

A, B and C – two lists will be prepared, referring to: new star clients and present star clients. First of all these clients will be actively contacted in order to present the company and subsequently to obtain work and projects.

D, E and F – marketing expenses (sponsorships, advertisements, stands in fairs, etc) will concentrate exclusively on the star and neutral segments. Nothing will be spent on the black segments.

G, H and I – as well as active commercial activity, passively generated requests will occur (eg by word of mouth). These opportunities will be treated in one of the three following ways::
- only exceptionally will orders be accepted from clients in the black segments – 1st situation;
- the decision to accept a request for orders by the other clients will always be analysed and considered in accordance with a list of certain criteria to be defined. After case-by-case analysis, the decision to make a proposal can take place (2nd situation);
- or not (3rd situation).

Figure 7.4 Implications of the three types of segments for an engineering services company

segments in terms of the company 's competitive position and/or attractiveness, while *black segments* are weak segments from the competitive point of view as well as attractiveness. By adding the competitive position to attractiveness, both on a scale of 1 to 5, the star segments obtain 10, 9, 8, the neutral 7, 6, 5 and the blacks 4, 3, or 2 (the sum of the values the segments acquire on the attractiveness and competitive position scale).[5]

In the example of an engineering services company, these three types of segments have different implications in terms of active commercial activity, of the marketing budget and the presentation of proposals. The differences can be schematically summarized as in Figure 7.4, where the clients on the star list (new or present) within the star segments will be the object of marketing budget expense and their purchases will be actively sought. Clients not on this list in the star segments and all the clients in the neutral segments will also be the object of marketing expense, but the opportunities for orders will emerge passively. After an analysis based on several criteria the decision whether or not to accept the order will be taken. No money from the marketing budget will be spent on clients in the black segments and only in exceptional cases will they be the object of sales by the company.

Also in the case in which it is decided to differentiate between these three kinds of segment, it is possible to evaluate the strategic reorientation (repositioning on the market) included in the strategic plan. If the strategic plan should indicate directions (segments) which fully *coincide* with the present strategy of the company, this is the same as saying once again that the strategic plan would indicate *continuing* with the company's *course*.

In this situation the company would (ideally) invoice:

- 2/3 (66 per cent) in segments which the strategic plan indicates are *stars*;
- 1/3 (34 per cent) in segments which the strategic plan indicates are *neutral*;
- nothing (0 per cent) in segments which the strategic plan indicates are black.[6]

For example, if the situation should be in fact divided as follows: 10.5 per cent in star segments, 84.5 per cent in neutral segments and 5 per cent in black segments, then the amount of strategic reorientation is given in Figure 7.5. This means that in order to capitalize to the maximum on the perspectives of sales volume, growth and advantages referring to competition the company should alter approximately (a little less than) half of its present position on the market. It should be noted that the differences in sales in the star and black segments are accentuated by a weight of two as it is dealing with extreme segments (either very attractive and where the company has competitive advantages, or not at all attractive and where the company does not have competitive advantage). The neutral segments are intermediate situations and therefore the differences are less important.

Figures 7.6, 7.7, 7.8 and 7.9 present four simulations for the formula in Figure 7.5, the example which is made with the simplest formula of strategic reorientation. As can be concluded from the simulation, the results of the formula vary as expected, between 0 per cent when the present situation is ideal (and therefore the strategic plan points in the direction of continuity) and nearly 100 per cent when the necessary amount of strategic orientation increases (when the present situation is 100 per cent of invoicing in the black segments, the index takes the value of 100 per cent).

	Segments		
	A Stars	B Neutral	C Black
1. If the strategy indicated by the strategic plan were equal to the present strategy of the company its invoicing would be distributed as follows:	66%	34%	0%
2. The present situation is:	10.5%	84.5%	5%
3. Difference in absolute value between 1 and 2	55.5%	50.5%	5%
4. Multiplication of 3A by 2, 3B by 1 and 3C by 2[1]	111%	50.5%	10%
5. Total (sum of 4A with 4B and 4C)		171.5	
6. The maximum of strategic reorientation would occur if the invoicing were distributed thus:	0%	0%	0%
7. Difference in absolute value between 1 and 6 (multiplied respectively by 2, 1 and 2)(1)	132%	34%	200%
8. Total (sum of 7A with 7B and 7C)		366%	
9. Amount of strategic reorientation (5/8)		$= \dfrac{171.5\%}{366} =$	46.9%

Note:[1] 2, 1 and 2 are the weights attributed to the difference between the ideal and the real invoicing in the star, neutral and black segments.

Formula

$$\%SR = \frac{|\%EA - \%EI| \times 2 + |\%NTA - \%NTI| \times 2 + |\%NGA - \%NGI| \times 2}{3.66}$$

Where
%SR = Percentage of strategic reorientation
%EA = Present percentage in the star segments
%NTA = Present percentage neutral segments
%NGA = Present percentage in the black segments
%EI = Ideal percentage in the star segments (66%)
%NTI = Ideal percentage in the neutral segment (34%)
%NGI = Ideal percentage in the black segment (0%)

Figure 7.5 Analysis of strategic reorientation implied by the strategic plan

	Segments		
	A Stars	B Neutral	C Black
1. Ideal situation	66.0%	34.0%	0.0%
2. Present situation	10.0%	30.0%	60.0%
3. Absolute error (1–2)	56.0%	4.0%	60.0%
4. Weighted absolute error	112.0%	4.0%	120.0%
5. Total weighed absolute error (4A + 4B + 4C)		236.0%	
6. Present extreme situation	0.0%	0.0%	100.0%
7. Maximum weighted absolute error	132.0%	34.0%	200.0%
8. Maximum total weighted absolute error (7A + 7B + 7C)		336.0%	
9. % strategic reorientation (5/8)		64.5%	

Figure 7.6 Examples of analysis, Hypothesis 1

	Segments		
	A Stars	B Neutral	C Black
1. Ideal situation	66.0%	34.0%	0.0%
2. Present situation	60.0%	5.0%	35.0%
3. Absolute error (1–2)	6.0%	29.0%	35.0%
4. Weighted absolute error	12.0%	29.0%	70.0%
5. Total weighed absolute error (4A + 4B + 4C)		111.0%	
6. Present extreme situation	0.0%	0.0%	100.0%
7. Maximum weighted absolute error	132.0%	34.0%	200.0%
8. Maximum total weighted absolute error (7A + 7B + 7C)		336.0%	
9. % strategic reorientation (5/8)		30.3%	

Figure 7.7 Examples of analysis, Hypothesis 2

	Segments		
	A Stars	B Neutral	C Black
1. Ideal situation	66.0%	34.0%	0.0%
2. Present situation	55.0%	40.0%	5.0%
3. Absolute error (1–2)	11.0%	6.0%	5.0%
4. Weighted absolute error	22.0%	6.0%	10.0%
5. Total weighed absolute error (4A + 4B + 4C)		38.0%	
6. Present extreme situation	0.0%	0.0%	100.0%
7. Maximum weighted absolute error	132.0%	34.0%	200.0%
8. Maximum total weighted absolute error (7A + 7B + 7C)		336.0%	
9. % strategic reorientation (5/8)		10.4%	

Figure 7.8 Examples of analysis, Hypothesis 3

	Segments		
	A Stars	B Neutral	C Black
1. Ideal situation	66.0%	34.0%	0.0%
2. Present situation	5.0%	45.0%	50.0%
3. Absolute error (1–2)	61.0%	11.0%	50.0%
4. Weighted absolute error	122.0%	11.0%	100.0%
5. Total weighed absolute error (4A + 4B + 4C)		233.0%	
6. Present extreme situation	0.0%	0.0%	100.0%
7. Maximum weighted absolute error	132.0%	34.0%	200.0%
8. Maximum total weighted absolute error (7A + 7B + 7C)		336.0%	
9. % strategic reorientation (5/8)		63.7%	

Figure 7.9 Examples of analysis, Hypothesis 4

CONCLUSION

The aim of this chapter was to introduce the concept of strategic reorientation and three ways of evaluating it. There are three advantages. First, by evaluation it is possible to see the amount of repositioning In the market the company needs to do in order to improve its situation in terms of efficiency. Assuming the strategic plan is well made, the degree of strategic reorientation it implies (which varies between 0 and 100 per cent) is an indicator of the present degree of the company 's inefficiency (maladjusted positioning in the market). The value of the strategic reorientation is thus an indicator of the company 's subordinate situation and its global underutilization of resources.

Then, as the internal organization[7] depends on the strategy, the greater the amount of necessary strategic orientation, the greater will be the necessary alterations to attain efficiency. The value of the strategic reorientation concept is that the amount of internal alterations needed to be made in the company to implement the new strategy as outlined by the strategic plan can be anticipated and prepared for.

Third, an internal reorganization is always a costly process (in time and money) and difficult. Before carrying it out it is useful to re-examine the strategic plan to be sure that there are no mistakes either in its assumptions or its conclusion. After this analysis, if the contents of the strategic plan are confirmed as valid then but only then should strategic reorientation be implemented.

If there is an indication of underutilization of resources, this is a warning of the need for internal reorganization and suggests a second check of the strategic plan. There are three advantages of evaluating strategic reorientation. It should be noted that this evaluation is dynamic, by contrast to the four evaluations of present strategy presented in Chapter 4, to the qualification of strategy in Chapter 5 and to the definition of mission in Chapter 6. These are all statistical evaluations and definitions as they refer only to a strategy, and it could be the present or intended one.

It is the difference between planning (which is dynamic) and the plan (which is static). As Heraclitus says, 'Everything flows and nothing stays.'[8] To change plans means the possibility of being able to preserve what is worthwhile (which is justified) and modifying the rest. There is nothing wrong in changing opinion, if it is for the better. It is worse to make mistakes about time in management than in grammar.

8

Conclusion

Tiananmen, August 1966: Mao Tse-tung salutes the Red Guard

INTRODUCTION

This last chapter summarizes the benefits of what has been achieved in this book: the definition of strategy and its measurement. Those advantages are threefold: coordination of effort; concentration of effort; and leadership knowledge of where one is; that is of one's present strategy. Those are the starting points from which strategic movements can be delineated *vis-à-vis* competitors, which is the task of the next book.

> *I have ten against one hundred, but I always attack ten against one. One hundred times. That way I win.*
>
> MAO TSE-TUNG

INDUSTRIES / POINT OF VIEW		ONE INDUSTRY	VARIOUS INDUSTRIES
S T R A T E G I C	QUANTITIVE TERMS	Chapter 4 (Quantification) 1. Concentration 2. Extension 3. Competitive position 4. Diversity	Chapter 3 (Strategic Plan) Vertical integration Diversity
	QUALITIVE TERMS	Chapter 5 (Typology) 1. Mink 2. Lynx 3. Horse 4. Lion	Chapter 6 Mission
DYNAMICS		Chapter 7 Concept of strategic reorientation	

Figure 8.1   Summary

This book began by searching for the concept of strategy at its origins – military art – and transplanted it into the economic area. Then the concept of strategy was worked on in close connection with tactics, and its various instruments were explored.

Chapter 3 showed how a strategic plan should be prepared and Chapters 4, 5, 6 and 7 evaluated the strategy: first quantifying it, then qualifying it; subsequently defining it (synthesizing) and finally evaluating it in dynamic terms, using the concept of strategic reorientation – see Figure 8.1.

All these aspects (preparation of the strategic plan and subsequent quantification, qualification, synthesis and evaluation of reorientation), compete for the company's effectiveness, that is, to do the right things, which is one of the necessary conditions for the good performance of organizations. Efficiency is essentially linked to quality in day-to-day management (a reason why management has already been defined as a series of interruptions constantly interrupted by interruptions). Three advantages result from quality of effectiveness.

The first is the existence of a common vision and coordination of efforts which originate from clarity of objectives. This clarity of objectives involves every aspect of the organization's activity, even when it is not perceived or apparently is not constantly present in the day-to-day work. As Sun Tzu said, 'Everyone can see the tactics I use to conquer, but no one can foresee the strategy on which my victory is based.' It is easier to organize the functional areas (marketing, production, finances, etc) when there is a clear idea of what has to be implemented.

The second advantage of a clear and detailed definition of the strategy, is that it enables the concentration[1] of effort, an objective which has always been argued for and pursued since the time of the scientists of antiquity (Archimedes), the military centuries ago (Frederick the Great, Clausewitz) and 20th-century soldiers (Mao Tse-tung), to the famous economists (Peter F Drucker) – see Table 8.1.

Table 8.1 Defence of concentration of efforts

Archimedes:
Give me somewhere to stand, and I will move the earth.

Frederick the Great:
He who defends everything, defends nothing.

Karl von Clausewitz:
In war few things are as important as placing our army so that instead of being weak in many places it is strong in few.

Mao Tse-tung:
I have ten against one hundred, but I always attack ten against one. One hundred times. That way I win.

Peter F Drucker:
The difference between successful and unsuccessful diversified companies is that the former have a core of unity whether it be technology or market.

Third, and last of all, clear knowledge of the strategy which the organization follows permits integral knowledge of the starting point from which the strategic movements can be delineated *vis-à-vis* competitors.

In the global village which is the world today no institution can survive if it is not competitive, and none will manage to be competitive if it commits strategic mistakes. As Darwin said, 'In the fight for survival not being strong (competitive) is almost like being guilty.'

This will be the theme of the next book in this series: which strategic movements an institution must follow, and when, based on a detailed knowledge of the present strategy (the task dealt with in this book). Strategists are like surgeons; their mistakes are usually fatal.

Appendix

EXAMPLES OF STRATEGIC PLANS

Example 1 Company Y's strategic plan

Geographical area: Belgium
Industry: Feminine hygiene and toilet articles

Company Y intends to establish itself in the industry of feminine hygiene and cleansing products: skin cleansers, toners, creams, soap and shampoos based on natural products, perfumes, deodorants, gel and bath foams.

Company's mission: Our business is feminine beauty.
Market segments in which Company Y is established: see Figure A.1

	Children (F)	Adolescents and Young Women up to 25 years	Young Women (over 25 and younger than 35)	Mature Women (over 35 and younger than 50)	Women over 50	Total
Class A			1 28%			28%
Class B			2 22%	4 38%		60%
Class C1			3 12%			12%
Class C2						
Class D						
Total			62%	38%		100%

The amounts mentioned in the table refer to the percentage of the company's invoicing in the corresponding segments.

> Segments in which the company is not represented

Figure A.1 Segmentation matrix of Company Y

The amounts mentioned in Figure A.1 refer to the percentage of the company's invoicing in the corresponding segments.

Segments in which the company is not present

First segment: Young women over 25 and younger than 35 in social class A

1.   Attractiveness of the segment:
     Growth Rate: 30 per cent
     Sales Volume: 2 billion dollars   } ROI = 17 per cent
     Profit margin per unit: 30 per cent
2.   Competitive position:

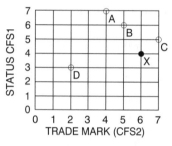
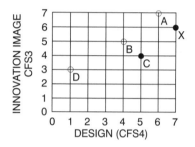

A, B, C and D = Main Competitions
Y = Original

Competitive Position of x=6.2%

Figure A.2 Critical factors of success Y segment 1

Strong points:
● commercialization of the product is done in its own shops, situated in excellent locations;
● image of the make;
● highly specialized service providing client with advice;
● manufacturing know-how and packaging design;
● manufacturer's guarantee.

Synergies
Estimated at approximately 22 per cent, in investment terms and production cost, due to:
● sharing of physical resources in production (warehouse, installations and transport);
● sharing of physical resources in staffing (juridical assessment, accounting, personnel and market research);

- sharing of intangible resources (make, image and copyright);
- sharing of distribution channels.

$$\text{Synergy} = 24,500 / 110,000 = 22 \text{ per cent}$$

Second segment: Young women over 25 and younger than 35 in social class B

1. Attractiveness of the segment:
    Growth rate: 25 per cent
    Sales Volume: 1,500,000,000   } ROI = 13 per cent
    Profit margin per unit: 25 per cent
2. Competitive position:

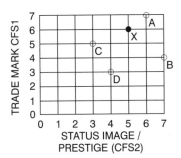 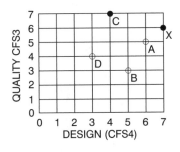

Competitive Position=16.1%

Figure A.3 Critical factors of success Y segment 2

Strong points:
- commercialization of the product is done in its own shops, situated in excellent locations;
- image of the make;
- highly specialized service providing client with advice;
- manufacturing know-how and packaging design;
- manufacturer's guarantee.

Synergies
Estimated at approximately 11 per cent, in investment terms and production cost, due to:
- sharing of physical resources in production (warehouses, installations and transport);
- sharing of physical resources in staffing (juridical assessment, accounting, personnel and market research);

- sharing of intangible resources (make, image and copyright);
- sharing of distribution channels.

$$\text{Synergy} = 15{,}500/145{,}000 = 11 \text{ per cent}$$

Third segment: Young women over 25 and younger than 35 in social class C1

1. Attractiveness of the segment:
    Growth rate: 20 per cent
    Sales Volume: 1,600,000,000   } ROI = 11 per cent
    Profit margin per unit: 20 per cent

2. Competitive position:

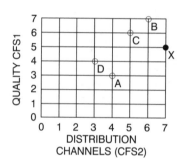 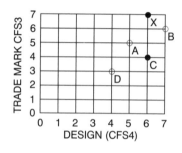

Competitive Position=17.2%

Figure A.4 Critical factors of success Y segment 3

Strong points:
- the company will produce some products (soap, gel and bath foam) at a competitive price (penetration price);
- in areas of less interest for the company, the adoption of the franchising system is envisaged;
- technical know-how in the design and conception of the packaging and product.

Synergies
Estimated at approximately 28 per cent, in investment terms and production cost, due to:
- sharing of physical resources in production (warehouse, installations and transport);

- sharing of physical resources in staffing departments (juridical assessment, accounting, personnel and market research);
- sharing of intangible resources (make, image and copyright);
- sharing of distribution channels.

$$\text{Synergy} = 22,500/80,000 = 28 \text{ per cent}$$

Fourth segment: Mature women over 35 and under 50 in social class B

1. Attractiveness of the segment:
   Growth rate: 30 per cent
   Sales Volume: 2,000,000,000
   Profit margin per unit: 25 per cent
   } ROI = 15 per cent

2. Competitive position:

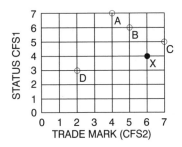 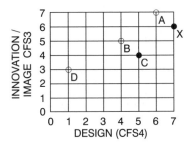

Competitive Position=18%

Figure A.5 Critical factors of success Y segment 4

Strong points:
- technical know-how for: products based on natural essences, creams for aging skins, toners;
- highly specialized service providing client with advice;
- commercialization of the product is done in its own shops, situated in excellent locations;
- image of the make;
- manufacturer's guarantee.

Synergies
Estimated at approximately 24 per cent, in investment terms and production cost, due to:

- sharing of physical resources in production (warehouses, installation and transport);
- sharing of physical resources in staffing (juridical assessment, accounting, personnel and market research);
- sharing of intangible resources (make, image and copyright);
- sharing of distribution channels.

$$\text{Synergy} = 35,000/145,000 = 24 \text{ per cent}$$

Example 2 Company Z's strategic plan

Geographical area: Belgium
Industry: Industrial hygiene and cleaning
Market segments in which Company Z is established: see Figure A.6

Treatment of the Floors **1**	Specialities **3**	Hand Care	Health Care
Machines Treatment of the Floors	Manual Accessories	Transport Cleaning Products **5**	Paper
Cleaners and Disinfectants for general use **2**	Kitchen Hygiene **4**	Clothes Washing	Provision of Serrvices

Note: 1, 2, 3, 4, and 5=segments which the company is present

Figure A.6 Segmentation matrix of Company Z

Needs	A	B	C	D	E	F	G	H	I	J	K	L
Clients												
Cleaning Companies												
Hotels												
Schools	1		2	3								
Restaurants						4						
Homes for the Aged												
Offices												
Health												
Canteens												
Catering Firms												
Car Manufacturers												
Concessionaires												
Garages												
Workshops								5				
Public Transport												
Lorry Washing												
Cistern Washing												

Note:

A Floor treatment
B Floor treatment machines
C Cleaners and disinfectants for general use
D Specialities
E Manual accessories
F Kitchen hygiene
G Hand care
H Cleaning products for transport
I Clothes washing
J Health care
K Paper
L Provision of services

Note: The following values given to the various companies in the Cartesian graphs
(critical factors of success), are mere examples, without any correspondence
to a real value.

Figure A.7 Segmentation of the industry

Cleaners and disinfectants

Table A.1 Floor treatment

Needs	Products	Clients
Preparation: Wooden floors Hard floors	Scourers	Cleaning Firms Hotels Schools
Protection: Wooden floors Hard floors	Wax Sealers Wash/polish	Restaurants Homes for the Aged Offices Health
Maintenance: Wooden floors Hard floors Fitted carpets	Detergents	

Table A.2 Attractiveness

Sales Volume	Growth Rate	Gross Margin	Average ROI next three years
2 200 000 thousand Escudos	2% per year	49%	18.5%

Complete line of
products + machinery + accessories

Technical knowledge of the
sales force

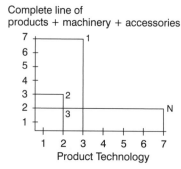

Note: 1 – Lever-Taski; 2 – Henkel; 3 – Triquimica; N – Us

Figure A.8 Competitive position = 50%

Table A.3 Synergy = 24.7%

Nature of Cost	Sales Force	Transport	Ware-house	Technical Services	Staff Depart-ments	Total
Real	96 000	17 000	15 000	0	55 000	183 000
Forecast	135 000	18 000	20 000	0	70 000	243 000
Synergy	29.0%	6.0%	25.0%	0.0%	21.0%	24.7%

Table A.4 Cleaners and disinfectants for general use

Needs	Products	Clients
Cleaning of interior surfaces (walls, tiles) Plastic, wood, windows, etc Remove grease from washable surfaces	General cleaners Ammoniacal cleaners Scaling cleaners Disinfectant cleaners Bacterial disinfectants	Cleaning Firms Hotels Schools Restaurants Homes for the Aged Offices Health
Disinfection of toilets and all washable surfaces	Grease-removing detergents Toilet freshener blocks	
Descaling of calcareous deposits	Urinal freshener blocks	
To avoid and eliminate unpleasant smells from toilets and urinals		

Table A.5 Attractiveness

Sales Volume	Growth Rate	Gross Margin	Average ROI next three years
1 200 000 thousand Escudos	4% per year	40%	9%

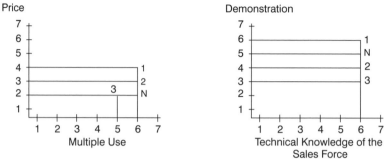

Note: 1 – Lever-Taski; 2 – Henkel; 3 – Johnson Wax Consumo; N – Us

Figure A.9 Competitive position = 0%

Table A.6 Synergy = 38.5%

Nature of Cost	Sales Force	Transport	Ware-house	Technical Services	Staff Depart-ments	Total
Real	8 700	5 500	1 400	0	5 000	20 600
Forecast	16 000	7 000	3 000	0	7 000	33 000
Synergy	46.0%	21.0%	53.0%	0.0%	33.0%	38.5%

Specialities

Table A.7 Specialities

Needs	Products	Clients
To clean and give a shine to furniture, plastic, formica, ceramics, leather, etc	Oils, Polishes (Liquids and Aerosols)	Cleaning Firms Hotels Schools Restaurants Homes for the Aged
Eliminate smells in the air	Atmosphere deodorants (liquids, gel, solids, aerosols, electrical devices)	Offices Health
Glass, windows and metal cleaning	Surface cleaners	
To repel and eliminate insects	Insecticides	

Table A.8 Attractiveness

Sales Volume	Growth Rate	Gross Margin	Average ROI next three years
1 300 000 thousand Escudos	5% per year	50%	20%

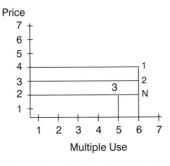

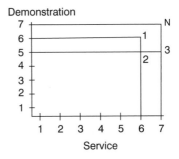

Note: 1 – Lever-Taski; 2 – Henkel; 3 – Johnson Wax Consumo; N – Us

Figure A.10 Competitive position = 15%

Table A.9 Synergy = 38.0%

Nature of Cost	Sales Force	Transport	Ware-house	Technical Service	Staff Depart-ments	Total
Real	9 100	200	1 500	0	5 300	16 100
Forecast	16 000	600	2 000	0	7 500	26 100
Synergy	43.0%	67.0%	25.0%	0%	29.0%	38.0%

Kitchen hygiene

Table A.10 Segment: Kitchen hygiene

Needs	Products	Clients
Manual washing up of crockery and kitchen implements	Washing up Grease removers Bactericide soaps	Hotels Restaurants Canteens Catering concerns Schools Homes for the Aged Health
Automatic washing up of crockery	Liquid detergents Dryer/Polisher Descaler Measures for detergents and dryers	
Cleaning of food area	Specific disinfectants Stainless steel cleaner Silver-cleaner Oven-cleaner	

Table A.11 Attractiveness

Sales Volume	Growth Rate	Gross Margin	Average ROI next three years
900 000 thousand Escudos	7.5% per year	40%	4%

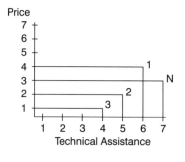

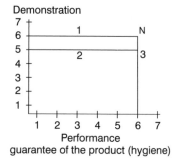

Note: 1 – Diversey; 2 – Lever-Taski; 3 – Henkel; N – Us

Figure A.11 Competitive position = 22%

Table A.12 Synergy = 28.0%

Nature of Cost	Sales Force	Transport	Ware-house	Technical Services	Staff Depart-ments	Total
Real	26 400	10 700	3 100	12 000	12 000	64 200
Forecast	40 000	13 000	6 000	15 000	15 000	89 000
Synergy	34 00	18.0%	48.0%	20.0%	20.0%	28.0%

Cleaning products for transport

Table A.13 Cleaning products for transport

Needs	Products	Clients
Exterior cleaning of vehicles	Detergent for chemical washing of vehicle bodywork	Car Manufacturers Concessionaires Gas Stations Garages
Cleaning of vehicles in washing tunnels and porticos	Car shampoo Dryer Waxes	Public Transport Lorry Washing Cistern Washing
Upholstery cleaning	Upholstery cleaners	
Removal of waxes and paraffin from new vehicles	Paraffin removers	
Engine washing	Cold emulsion/grease remover	
Cleaning of dashboards	Polyvinyl and synthetic cleaners	
Engine cooler	Anti-freeze	

Table A14 Attractiveness

Sales Volume	Growth Rate	Gross Margin	Average ROI next three years
700 000 thousand Escudos	5% per year	48%	19%

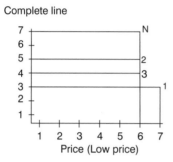

Note: 1 – Triquímica; 2 – Khiel; 3 – Petrochem; N – Us

Figure A.12 Competitive position = 19%

Table A.15 Synergy = 31.0%

Nature of Cost	Sales Force	Transport	Ware-house	Technical Services	Staff Depart-ments	Total
Real	14 800	5 700	2 300	6 000	8 700	37 500
Forecast	22 000	7 500	4 000	9 000	12 000	54 500
Synergy	33.0%	24.0%	43.0%	33.0%	28.0%	31.0%

Notes

A note to the reader; A book on strategic management with a war title?

1. In some cases, they seem even to be reversing their previous military fate by economic means; the acquisitions of Chrysler by Daimler-Benz and Rolls-Royce by Volkswagen are recent examples of this.

Chapter 1 Hannibal in Cannae

1. Our word *decimate* comes from a Roman practice. If a defeat or victory occurred and a general considered his army had not behaved sufficiently bravely, he ordered it to form ranks in an open field after the battle and a draw was made for one in every ten to be killed.
2. That was mainly Varro's opinion. During the time of the consuls it was the practice to command on alternate days.
3. From then on Rome started to recruit many of its best cavalry from the Gauls.
4. If the Carthaginian centre collapsed it would mean the defeat of the Carthaginian army divided into two.
5. According to Tito Livio (*The History of Rome*, Book 22), Cipian the Tribune formed two new legions based on them. They were more necessary than ever for the protection of Rome.
6. Namely, change of side of the Italians who did not have citizenship of Rome.
7. It should be remembered that the Parthenon, temple of Athena, had the inscription *Nosce te ipsum* (know yourself) on its portal.
8. It is one of the rare occasions when a smaller army managed to *encircle* a larger army.
9. An interesting question is whether the war in business is between companies or countries. Between companies there is obviously a war in their fight for the conquest of markets. And each country tries to promote its own national companies or those multinational companies that are controlled to a greater or lesser degree by its nationals as shareholders or managers or a mixture of both. That is quite simple. There is no real political independence if a country has only minimal control of its economic fabric. If a country has 70–80 per cent of its GDP controlled by foreign companies and on top of that a large part of them are from only one or two countries, its political independence is theoretical. All over the world there are popular sayings describing this. In Sicily, 'When the money plays, the people dance.' In the USA, 'When money talks, people listen.' In Russia, 'He whose bread I eat, his is the song I sing.'

Ironically enough some of the countries which were military defeated in the past seem to be reversing their fate by economic means: for instance, German companies Daimler and Volkswagen acquired recently American and British companies Chrysler and Rolls-Royce. Therefore there are many authors who argue that with the globalization of markets ('World Inc.') most countries are now at war. Economics, but war. Business is today what Clausewitz formerly said about war. It is the continuation of politics by other means.

Chapter 2 Strategy and tactics

1. The term 'strategy' comes from the Greek *strategos*, a civil and military governor of a province.

2. von Clausewitz, Karl (1978) *Von Kriege*, Penguin Classics.

3. The first book on military strategy dates from the 4th century AD – *The Art of War* by Sun Tzu.

4. To ask which business administration area is more important makes as much sense as to ask which wing of an airplane is most important, or which tyre of a car we no longer need. Left? Right? Rear? Front? That is why there is an old military saying that *there are no victories in strategy,* meaning strategy is never a *sufficient* condition for success but solely a *necessary* one, a prerequisite. Without good tactics, excellence in strategy usually falls short of delivering. On the other hand, if you excel in tactics but do not complement that with a sound strategy, you may win battles but you will lose the war. That is, you will never achieve long-term results and excellence.

5. Today many books on operational areas use the word 'strategy' for marketing purposes. A book which previously would have been called simply 'financial management' nowadays has the title 'strategic financial management'; and production management now appears on the market as strategic production management, and so on. This is a simple technique to sell more (books) which is associated with the popularity of the term 'strategy' (a concept whose use has developed during the last two decades). All subjects have their myths, but the more seriously we take them, the less we should become involved.

6. Until then the subject was called Business Policy or Management Policy and was based on case studies which attempted to analyse problems of coordination between the operational areas of management (marketing, finance, etc). The field of strategy had very few concepts, theories and autonomous techniques.

7. It is significant that in 1943, when Peter Drucker, then Professor of Philosophy in New York University, was invited by Alfred Sloan, President of General Motors, to do some consulting work, the former went to the New York Municipal Library and in the index tried to find which books were available on the subject of management. There were few and all were on the operational areas of accounting, financial management, taxation and

engineering; that is, production management. There was nothing about personnel, marketing and information systems of management and certainly nothing about strategy. All this has been developed since the 1940s.

8. In the remainder of this book the word 'market' will be used as a synonym for industry or geographical area.

9. Banks have always been special institutions. They have four types of potential clients: active companies, passive companies, active individuals, passive individuals. Most other institutions only have active clients. Bank clients can be persons or companies, while other institutions either sell industrial goods (the clients are usually companies) or consumable goods (the clients are persons). The strategic decisions of the banks must be based on two segmentation matrices: one for the retail bank and another for the corporate bank. The most usual segmentation matrix for the retail bank is presented in Figure 2.7, in which the two dimensions are the social class and the life-cycle phase.

10. Special situations are excluded in which for cultural, social and/or ethical reasons the entrepreneur opts for a certain industry/geographical area. The situation should then be seen in terms of the company trying to maximize profit subject to this type of restriction.

11. On this subject see Vasconcellos e Sá, J and Amaral, MC (1996) *The Modern Alchemists*, Instituto do Emprego e Formação Profissional, Lisbon, which has a chapter on the establishment of objectives for a company's business units.

12. It also aimed to be the beer to drink at the weekends (as the slogan says, 'It is good to drink something better at the weekends, isn't it?').

13. Like Marlboro for cigarettes.

14. Justifying the motto to be adopted in its sponsorship: 'Tell me who you live with, and I will tell you who you are.'

15. An interesting question is *whether tactics also influence strategy*. For instance, if Hannibal's army had been composed mainly of sailors it would have had to follow another strategy: to attack the Roman fleet in the Mediterranean. In business, if a firm lacks a certain raw material or cannot find a specifically skilled labour force, certain market segments (strategies) are precluded. In such instances, tactics also seem to influence strategy. Two aspects, however, are noteworthy. First, in these situations tactics exert *a veto rule* over strategy; that is, they veto some strategies but they do not indicate *which* strategy to follow. That is considerably different from the influence of strategy upon tactics since (as previous examples illustrate) strategy does indeed determine in a narrow sense the tactics to follow; what sales promotion should be, what advertising should be, what type of service should be offered, etc. Second, the cases where one starts by drawing a strategy and then after defining the tactics one concludes that the former must be reviewed are very rare – since they mean that very important and totally unpredictable events occurred after defining the strategy and before implementing it. Another explanation is that the strategy was badly formulated in the first place. The reason is simple. One of the criteria when evaluating alternative strategies is an organization's (or army's) strengths or special qualities. Therefore, only if these

were not considered at all, or were wrongly evaluated is it necessary to conclude that a given strategy cannot be implemented.

16. See the very interesting article on this subject by David L Hoyer (1990) 'Corestates New Jersey National Bank Markets to the Affluent by Shunning Mass Marketing', *Bank Marketing*, November.

17. As is demonstrated by Lone Star, which was adapted to the taste of Texas.

18. Segmentation raises very interesting questions, such as how to segment an industry and how far it should be taken (how many segments create an industry). For these procedural aspects, see Vasconcellos e Sá, J and Amaral, MC (1996) *The Modern Alchemists*, Instituto do Emprego e Formação Profissional, Lisbon. For space reasons only aspects of contents (and not process) are focused upon here.

19. It is easy to understand why. At one extreme, if there are as many companies as strategic groups, there will be a ratio of one to one, which would mean that each company would follow a specific behaviour (strategy) within the industry. There should be no reasons concerning the interrelation among the segments which would make one enterprise that is in segment X to go into segment Y. Entry into other segments would be dictated by attractiveness and strong points of the company, and not the synergetic relationship between the segments.

20. This analysis is, *ceteris paribus*, in terms of attractiveness; that is, with the exception of the case when the enterprise is already present these segments would be less attractive than segments empty at the moment. In any case the segments where enterprise C is alone are probably among the most synergetic together with those where the enterprises C and D are together.

21. Banks have enlarged their services to the area of insurance, in addition to offering a panoply of financial products; auditing companies have enlarged their activity to services of taxation, bookkeeping, recruitment of personnel, etc, all within consultancy and so on (see Figure 2.16).

22. A third type of strategy is that which the managers sometimes think they have and which has nothing to do with reality or present strategy. As W Rogers says, 'The problem with some people is not that they do not know, but that what they think they know in fact does not correspond to the truth. It is the difference between conscious ignorance and unconscious ignorance.'

Chapter 3 How to prepare a strategic plan

1. Either of the assets or share capital.

2. A good book on market studies or a basic book on strategy will provide several methods of estimating the sales, margin and growth rate of a segment. That is why no analysis is made here.

3. One of the humorous definitions of statistics is: 'The science according to which, if I eat a chicken and you do not eat anything, we have, on average,

eaten half a chicken each'.

4. For example, see Vasconcellos e Sá, J (1988) 'The impact of key success factors on company performance', *Long Range Planning*, December.

5. In order to estimate the critical factors of success and strong points see Vasconcellos e Sá, J and Hambruck, D (1989) 'Key success factors: Test of a general theory in the mature industrial product sector', *Strategic Management Journal*, **10**; and 'How to find critical success factors' in Vasconcellos e Sá, J and Amaral, MC (1996) *The Modern Alchemists*, Instituto do Emprego e Formação Profissional, Lisbon.

6. If a cross-section regression is made of the companies' profits in a segment on 30 to 40 variables (service, distribution, etc), the critical factors of success are those variables which vary with statistically significant regression coefficients.

7. The values given to any of these companies are merely examples to illustrate the text and are not intended to pronounce any judgement of real value on them.

8. There are two basic methods to evaluate the strong points of an institution: the Delphi technique and the technique of secondary data. See Vasconcellos e Sá, J and Amaral, MC (1996) *The Modern Alchemists*, Instituto do Emprego e Formação Profissional, Lisbon.

9. The next chapter will present an alternative way to measure a firm's competitive position, based not on its qualities (strengths) in the key success factors, but on its market share. As will be shown, the two measures of competitiveness can be expected to be closely correlated. That correlation constitutes a measure of the accuracy of the evaluation of the key success factors or the strengths or both.

10. Some authors have recently pretended that one should speak of consumer advantage rather than competitive advantage; the reason being that otherwise 'one could have a competitive advantage and the consumer couldn't care less'. The prudent thinker can easily detect why that is not so. Competitive advantage comes from having strengths *in the key success factors*, not merely from having strengths. Since key success factors are those tasks which are most important to customers *there can be no competitive advantage without consumer advantage*. If this is true, why do some authors pretend to make a distinction between consumer and competitive advantage? Simply put, it is a reasoning mistake created by eagerness to be innovative. Ambition without substance (which comes from the maturing of time and tranquil thought) leads to blunt errors, such as this, and to unnecessary confusion.

11. The first time history tells us about this concept being openly used is in Rome, 494 BC. In that year, protesting against their lack of economic and political rights, the common people of Rome massed together and marched out of the city. They went to a nearby hill and declared their intention to found a new city on that spot. The Roman patricians who remained behind soon began to wonder who would work in the fields and the workshops, and who

would serve in the army. In an effort to persuade the commoners to return to their former tasks, so the legend goes, they sent a certain Menenius Agrippa to negotiate. Aggripa approached their camp and spoke thus:

> In old days, when the various organs of the body used to speak to one another, the hands, the mouth and the teeth decided to revolt, claiming that they did all of the work of eating, but only the stomach received the benefit. So the hands refused to pick up anything, the mouth refused to open and the teeth refused to chew. By and by the body grew hungry, it weakened and withered – the whole body, including the hands, the mouth and the teeth.

In this way, the common people realized that even though only the stomach appeared to benefit from eating, in fact, the entire body works together, each organ performing its own role, producing a benefit which is shared by all. And so they saw that global welfare depends upon the cooperation of individual parts.

12. Here two aspects should be noted. First, as well as saving of costs and also higher sales due to control of the distribution channels, synergy can refer to higher prices (through transfer of the image of one segment to another) and greater investment. Second, synergy can be negative. To simplify and to concentrate on the essential both these aspects of analysis and calculation have been excluded, although the procedure in its essence is the same. For a method of calculating the synergy between two segments of the market, for example, see Vasconcellos e Sá, J (1989) 'A practical way to evaluate synergy', in *The Handbook of Business Strategy*, Macmillan.

13. A simpler measure of synergy is provided by lay-offs which frequently result from mergers. Recently, for instance, the CEOs of Union des Banques Suisses and Societé des Banques Suisses announced that, as a consequence of fusing their operations, they were planning to lay off 13,000 employees in a combined workforce of 56,000. The resulting synergy is therefore $13/56 = 23$ per cent. Naturally, that is synergy solely in personnel, to which other sources of synergy could eventually be added in installations, equipment, market penetration and so on.

14. A segmentation matrix must be dedicated to the target geographical area, however small it might be, even when it is a sub-group of a country. However, a practical question is posed when the zone of activity is enlarged. Within a country how many geographical zones (and therefore regional segmentation matrixes) should be made?

   What should be considered an autonomous geographical area, for the purposes of presentation of a segmentation matrix? A federal country? One of the states within this federation? Or an autonomous region? If a segmentation matrix is a combination of groups of clients, each with its specifications, in a specific space, in pragmatic terms a segmentation matrix should be made for all the regions with one or more of the following characteristics:
   • political and administrative autonomy;

- existence of barriers or customs differences (quotas, etc), techniques (norms and regulations with which the products must conform) and taxes (specific taxes either in the amount, or the incidence, or in the rate);
- cultural differences: Galicia, the Basque Country and Catalonia in Spain; Wallonia and Flanders in Belgium, etc.

Only when these three aspects together justify it should a region be considered autonomous and a segmentation matrix be made exclusively for it. In practice, political boundaries and autonomous administrative contours (which usually correspond to cultural specifics and barriers) are good guides. In any case, the segmentation matrix must correspond to the target geographical zone. What can happen is that within a country various segmentation matrixes can be made for its various regions. There will be as many matrixes (within the country) as the strength of the presence of the factors given above.

15. António Vieira (major scholar of the seventeenth century) wrote something similar in one of his letters to the Portuguese King D João IV: 'Forgive me, Your Highness, for such a long letter but I didn't have the ability to make it shorter.'

16. For each geographical area. If the company is in two or three geographical areas, the number of pages is duplicated or triplicated, but the process is essentially the same.

17. That is a well-accepted management principle: memos and documents should be kept complete but short. That requires sticking to the essential and is well known as the KISS principle: keep it short and simple. When KISS number one is not fulfilled, then comes KISSS number two (with one more s): keep it short and simple, stupid. It is not only a question of shortness of time to write and to read. More than that, it is a question of the importance of the document: the greater its importance, the less any secondary aspects (not to mention trivia) should hide or distract one's attention from its essential core. Synthesis is a common characteristic of most important statements: Pythagorus' theorem has 24 words; Archimedes' principle, 67; the Ten Commandments, 179; and the American declaration of independence, 300. From synthesis follows simplicity, which is one of the major tenets of all great advertisements and marketing slogans. They are simple. Seven Up: the uncola; WLKM: the unrock station; etc. Why is it then, that most strategic plans (and other documents) are neither short, nor simple? The answer is that in life, what is difficult is to simplify; what is simple is to create difficulties.

18. This type of strategic plan hinders the life of the firm. They make people lose time (in the preparation of useless plans) instead of dealing with the day-to-day functions of management and cause a loss of prestige as they present an image to persons outside the company that it has no clear orientation.

19. There are those who argue that survival instincts are stronger than profit as objectives of the companies. But it is a false proposition as survival is a nec-

essary condition for profits. There can be no profit if there is no survival. However, companies do not want to survive just to survive. They want to do so in order to make profits. Therefore survival is not an end in itself but a means for profit. Once again, a comparison is useful here. It is what happens to people with regards to happiness and breathing. To be happy is the ultimate objective (even those who commit suicide do it because they think they will be happier than if they live). But to be happy it is necessary to breathe. However, the purpose of breathing is not just to survive but also to live well, to be happy. The happiness of companies is profit. The aim of profit must be understood in the medium and long term as frequently there is a trade-off between the maximization of profit in the short term and its optimization in the medium and long term.

20.   Values and moral norms can be understood as restrictions which frame and format the pursuit of profit. The greater the number and more limited these amounts, the less free is the field of action remaining in the pursuit of profit. In non-profit-making companies – for example, a foundation with cultural and sponsorship activities – the characteristics and role of the strategic plan are the same. This type of institution has objectives which are equivalent to profit: maximization of efficiency (to offer services and activities to which society gives great value) and efficiency (to do it at low cost). That is to do the right thing in the right way. The two concepts together are the equivalent of profit.

21.   On this subject, see Mintzberg, H (1993) *The Rise and Fall of Strategic Planning*, Macmillan.

22.   An important side question is the temporal dimension of a strategic plan, namely: how often should it be reviewed; and what should be its time horizon in years (one, two, five, ten, one hundred?) Regarding the first question, the norm is that strategic plans should be reviewed yearly (like other documents such as the cash budgets, the forecast income statements and balance sheets). When the firm is small and the environment stable, then a two-year periodicity to review the plan should do. As for the time horizon of a strategic plan, as Rosabeth Moss Kanter has put it: it does not matter, provided you review it each year (or every two years, or…).

Chapter 4 Quantifying strategy

1.   Most of the existing strategy evaluations refer to inter-industry relationships, eg relatedness, vertical interconnection, technological diversification and market.

2.   As they are technological incongruities.

3.   Both the Gini coefficient and the Lorenz curve are easy to calculate. See a good book on statistics on this subject, such as Murteira, B and Black, G (1983) *Descriptive Statistics*, McGraw-Hill. Basically the Gini coefficient is

equal to

$$\frac{1 - \sum_{i=1}^{m-1} qi}{\sum_{i=1}^{m-1}}$$

where m is the number of classes, pi the proportion of sales accumulated until the amount, 1 and qi the proportion of the total of the accumulated segments until i.

4. Degree of concavity of the curve in relation to x-axis and the ordinates.

5. If, for example, concentration is 0.6, since the extension curve is below that of concentration, that curve is equal or bigger than 0.6. Therefore the extension ratio is equal or smaller than 0.4 (1 minus the value of the curve).

6. Including the last segment contained in the accumulated bar.

7. As a consequence, the best way to evaluate the competitive position is through cumulative relative market share; the second best way is through cumulative absolute market share; the third and fourth ways are through simple market share, either absolute or relative.

8. As a consequence, there are two different ways to assess a firm's competitive advantage: through its rating in the key success factors relative to competition (as discussed in Chapter 3); and through market share (relative or absolute), as discussed here. An interesting question arises as to what should we expect the relation between these two measures to be. And what do exceptions, when they occur, mean? The answer to the first question is straightforward: we would expect both measures of competitiveness to be strongly associated. That is, if the measure based on key factors indicate +30 per cent, for example, the value indicated by the relative market share should be similar. And vice versa. And when there is a strong discrepancy between the measures (say key factors indicate +20 per cent and relative market share -10 per cent)? If we assume clients are seldom wrong in such a case, the conclusion can only be either the key success factors or the strengths or both were badly estimated. A main exception exists: when the firm is new in the market segment and its qualities are still not well known to customers. In any case, a good test of the accuracy/quality of our estimation of strengths and success factors can be performed by comparing the index of competitiveness based on those concepts and the index of competitiveness based on market share. How similar are they?

9. The value 1 is the minimum of diversity when the company is in two or more segments. When the company in the industry is just in one segment then the specialization is total and the diversity is of course zero.

10. As the proverb says, 'The more we talk the less the others remember.' The

advantage of quantifying strategy (conciseness) could be called the Getúlio Vargas principle, after the ex-president of Brazil who was noted for his brevity in a country where that is rare. One day at the end of a banquet, a minister's wife approached him and said, 'Mr President, I wagered with my friends that I would manage to get you to say more than two words.' Gertúlio Vargas replied simply, 'You lost.'

11. Simplicity is always an advantage and rather difficult to obtain. I think it was Professor Dias Marques who – when a member of my family approached him and said he had read one of his books and was agreeably surprised with its simplicity – replied, 'Thank you. You have no idea the work that gave me.'

12. Using the segments where concentration takes place as a reference, the competitive position will improve, etc.

Chapter 5 Qualifying strategy

1. Valverde, N (1983) 'Developing profitable strategies that don't box you in', *Bank Marketing*, June.

2. It is a bare product, without frills or extras. It would be a white product, if it were not for the trade mark. Companies following this type of strategy can be found in any industry (see Figure 5.4).

3. For some time Cray Computers considered the hypothesis of entering the mini-supercomputers segment but, after analysis, decided against it and continued with its specialization in supercomputers.

4. The size, perfume and all the other aspects referring to the basic contents remain the same.

5. Subsequently both follow the horse strategy.

6. See Chapters 3 and 4.

7. Basically, while in the strategy of lion there is a one-to-one relationship between the models and the market segments the firm is in, in the horse strategy the number of models is smaller than that of market segments. It can therefore be said that a strategy has more and more of horse as the ratio of the number of models to number of segments decreases; and there is a negative correlation between this ratio and the presence of economies of scale in the industry: the lower the ratio, the greater the economies of scale.

8. The choice between mink and lynx is direct. It has to do with the criteria indicated in Chapter 3: attractiveness and competitive position and, when a company is in more than one segment, synergy.

9. There are two interesting marginal aspects. First, the intensity of the horse strategy is evaluated by: numbers of models offered divided by number of segments. This varies between $1/N$ and N, N being the number of segments served. The difference between the lion and horse strategies can consequently be measured by $(N - X)/N$, where X equals the number of models

and N the number of segments). Second, what characterizes the lion and horse strategies is that the number of models is less than or equal to the number of segments (as it is defined as a lion strategy when they are equal and as a horse strategy when the models are fewer). The greater the ratio of segments to models, the greater the economies of scale and the less the differentiation of the product/satisfaction given the client/margin/price.

10. Using a matrix, the correlation comes as shown:

Qualitative Measures:	Lynx	Mink	Horse	Lion
Quantitative Measures				
Concentration	+	+	–	–
Extension	–	–	+	+
Diversity	–	–	+	+
Competitiveness	0	0	0	0

Chapter 6 Summarizing strategy

1. For which you can choose to opt or not, but that is a decision to be taken after periodic analysis.

2. See the interesting article in the *Harvard Business Review*, March-April 1986, called: 'Porsche on Nichemanships', regarding the specific needs satisfied by a Porsche (as opposed to other types of luxury cars, such as Lotus or Ferrari).

3. Who buy electrical equipment for the kitchens of the flats they have for sale and thereby transmit an image of comfort and readiness for occupation.

4. Entry into the Italian market was only attempted as from the middle of the 1980s.

5. Using Atlanta as the centre of its transfer system, having 40 to 50 planes on the ground 10 times a day.

6. That is why Boeing, for example, has so many different types of plane: the 707 for the intercontinental market (competing with the Comet 4, the VC-10 and the Convair 990); the 720 for the continental market, the competition for which is the Comet 3, the Convair 880 and the DC8 10/20; the 727 for medium-haul routes, where it mainly competes with the Trident 1–3; the 737 for short hauls in which the competitors are the DC9; Bac III and F–28, etc.

7. Objectives (priority tasks) and marketing are *tactical* areas. The *strategic* square (product, need, etc) is, obviously, strategic. Therefore changes in tactical areas as a consequence of change in strategy are further examples of how tactics depend upon strategy, just as Chapter 2 indicated.

8. By contrast, Honda defined its need as transportation and therefore continuously upgraded its motorcycles and cars by launching new models of greater power and price, as well as other transportation vehicles: vans, all-terrain vehicles, buses, and so on.

9. The rule is that each strategic square or business area must benefit from the

specific attention of a business unit (SBU). That is, a one-to-one relationship must exist between them, without prejudicing the mechanisms of coordination between them, of course.

10. This indicator of synergy is ordinal. The indicator presented in Chapter 4 (diversity) is also ordinal. The indicator presented in Chapter 3 (costs saved divided by total costs) is cardinal. There are therefore three ways to measure synergy, just as there are two ways of measuring a firm's competitiveness: through its rating in the key success factors, and through market share.

11. The reader who is not very interested in these matters can go directly to Chapter 7 without losing the basic structure of the book.

12. 'The big power of little ideas', *Harvard Business Review*, May-June 1964.

13. As mentioned in Chapter 3, when referring to the 'Principles to be followed in a strategic plan'.

14. Strategic business unit. This is a division of a company which can be evaluated by a separate profit budget or ROI, which has a general manager up front to whom various functional areas report.

15. On the corporate level, each sub-mission includes in its turn several missions on the business level.

16. To define the objectives of each SBU within each strategic square, see Vasconcellos e Sá, J and Amaral, MC (1996) *The Modern Alchemists*, Instituto do Emprego e Formação Profissional, Lisbon.

Chapter 7 Strategic reorientation

1. Basically, strategic reorientation corresponds to the concept of apprenticeship in an institution. One day when a disciple remarked to Ghandi that he had said something different the previous week, he just replied that he had learnt it since then.

2. To do the correct things in contrast to efficiency (to do things correctly).

3. Adaptation given the perspectives in terms of sales volumes, growth and competitive position of the firm with respect to the competition.

4. For simplicity in the subsequent analysis it is assumed that the geographical area remains unaltered. If this is not the case, the logic of the analysis would not be subsequently altered, and only this new variable would have to be taken into account.

5.

Position of the firm		*Attractiveness of the segment*
Strong	- 5 -	Upper
Strong/Reasonable	- 4 -	Upper/Average
Reasonable	- 3 -	Average
Reasonable/Weak	- 2 -	Average/Lower
Weak	-1 -	Lower

6. Given the cellular metabolism of a company, in terms of segments which are abandoned and new segments where it ventures, this distribution of invoic-

ing is less extreme than expecting the firm to invoice 100 per cent in star segments.

7. Structure, control systems, management information system, personnel training, etc.

8. Buddha has a similar phrase, 'Nothing constant exists, except change.'

Chapter 8 Conclusion

1. Different from coordination, which means articulation (between the various members of the company). Concentration means greater selectivity in the choice of fields of activity.

.

Further reading

Aaker, DA (1984) *Developing Business Strategies*, John Wiley & Sons

Aaker, DA (1988) *Strategic Market Management*, John Wiley & Sons

Aaker, DA and Day, GS (1986) 'The perils of high-growth markets', *Strategic Management Journal*, September/October

Abel, DF (1979) *Defining the Business: The Strategic Point of Strategic Planning*, Prentice-Hall

Albert, KJ (1983) *The Strategic Management Handbook*, McGraw-Hill

Andrews, KA (1980) *The Concept of Corporate Strategy*, Irwin

Ansoff, HI (1967) *Corporate Strategy*, McGraw-Hill

Ansoff, HI (1988) *The New Corporate Strategy*, John Wiley & Sons

Ansoff, HI (1990) *Implanting Strategic Management*, Prentice-Hall

Brache, AP (1992) 'Process improvement and management: A toll for strategic implementation', *Planning Review* special issue, International Strategic Management Conference, September/October

Business Week (1984) 'The new breed of strategic planners', September

Campbell, A (1992) 'The power of mission: Aligning strategy and culture', *Planning Review* special issue, International Strategic Management Conference, September/October

Carr, LP (1992) 'Applying cost of quality to a service business', *Sloan Management Review*

Chan, YL and Lynn, BE (1993) 'Hierarchical analysis as a means od evaluating tangibles and intangibles of capital investments', *Mid-Atlantic Journal of Business*, March

Christensen, CR., Andrews, KR and Bower, JL (1978) *Business Policy: Text and Cases*, Irwin

Clark, C and Brennan, K (1993) 'Global mobility: The concept', *Long Range Planning*, December

Cooper, RG (1994) 'Debunking the myths of new product development', *Research-Technology Management*, July/August

Cooper, RG and Kleinschmidt, EJ (1993) 'Screening new products for potential winners', *Long Range Planning*, December

Curhan, RC and Kopp, R (1988) 'Obtaining retailer support for trade deals: Key success factors', *Journal of Advertising Research*, December 1997/January

Day, G (1993) 'New directions for corporations: Conditions for successful renewal', *European Management Journal*, June

Deffrages, EH, Ellis, PA, Treat, JE and Waite, AL 'E & P opportunities for service firms about in the CIS', *Oil & Journal*

Drucker, PF (1964) 'The big power of little ideas', *Harvard Business Review*, May/June

Drucker, PF (1986) *Inovação e Gestão*, Editorial Presença

Drucker, PF (1986) *The Practice of Management*, Harper & Row

Fadum, O *et al* (1993) 'Expert systems in action', *Pulp & Paper*, April

Gardner, JR, Rachlner, R and Sweeney, HWA (1986) *Handbook of Strategic Planning*, John Wiley & Sons

Glueck, WF and Jauch, LR (1984) *Business Policy and Strategic Management*, McGraw-Hill

Goold, M, Campbell, A and Luchs, K (1993) 'Strategies and styles revisited: "Strategic control" – Is it tenable?', *Long Range Planning*, December

Gugler, P (1992) 'Building transnational alliances to create competitive advantage', *Long Range Planning*, **25**, 1, pp 90–99

Hamill, J and Hunt, G (1993) 'Joint ventures in Hungary: Key success factors', *European Management Journal*

Hardy, KG (1986) 'Key success factors for manufacturers' sales promotion in package goods', *Journal of Marketing*, July

Harran, JM (1994) 'The ECR state of mind', *Progressive Grocer*, January

Hartley, RF (1991) *Management Mistakes and Successes*, 3rd edn, John Wiley & Sons

Heering, JP (1992) 'The role of intelligence in formulating strategy', *Journal of Business Strategy*, September/October

Hilligoss, RS (1992) 'Maintenance... The business opportunity of the 1990s', *Industrial Management*, March/April

Hunter, D (1993) 'Competition drives innovation and worldwide sourcing in fine chemicals', *Chemical Week*, October

Javidon, M (1995) 'Where planning fails: An exhaustive survey', *Long Range Planning*, **18**

Koontz, O'Donnel and Weihrich (1984) *Management*, McGraw-Hill

Kotler, P (1980), *Marketing Management: Analysis, Planning and Control*, 4th edn, Prentice-Hall

Lant, TK, Milliken, FJ and Batra, B (1992) 'The role of managerial learning and interpretation in strategic persistence and reorientation: An empirical exploration', *Strategic Management Journal*, **13**, pp 585–608, November

Lee, M and Son, B (1993) 'Korean strategies for export markets', *Long Range Planning*, December

Lendrevie, J *et al* (1992) *Teoria e Prática do marketing*, Gestão e Inovação, Publicações D Quixote

Lewis, JD (1992) 'The new power of strategic alliances', *Planning Review* special issue, International Strategic Management Conference, September/October

Lopez de Arriortua, JA (1993) 'Winning the third industrial revolution', *Executive Speeches*, June/July

Lowestein, MC (1986) 'The failure of strategic planning', *Journal of Business Strategy*, **6**, pp 75–80, Spring

Lucas Jr, HC (1986) *Information Systems Concepts for Management*, McGraw-Hill

Magrath, AJ (1994) 'Rethinking your strategy', *Sales and Marketing Management*, May

Melum, MM (1989) 'Total quality management: Steps to success', *Hospitals*, December

Mitchell, RE (1994) 'From adviser to business partner', *CA Magazine*, March

Mockler, RJ and Dologite, DG (1988) 'Developed-based systems for strategic corporate planning', *Long Range Planning*, February

Moriarty, DD (1992) 'Strategic information system planning for health service providers, *Health Care Management Review*, Winter

Newmam, WH and Logan, JP (1978) *Strategy, Policy and Central Management*, South Western

Ohinata, Y (1994) 'Benchmarking: The Japanese experience', *Long Range Planning*, August

Ohmae (1982) *The Mind of the Strategist*, McGraw-Hill

Porter, ME (1980) *Competitive Strategy: Techniques for Analyzing Industries and Competition*, Free Press

Porter, ME (1985) *Competitive Advantage: Creating and Sustaining Superior Performance*, Free Press

Porter, ME (1986) *Competition in Global Industries: Research Colloquy*, Harvard Business School Press

Porter, ME (1987) 'From competitive advantage to corporate strategy', *Harvard Business Review*, **65**, 3, pp 43–599

Porter, ME (1990) *The Competitive Advantage of Nations*, Macmillan

Raz, T (1993) 'Introduction of the project management discipline in a software development organization', *IBM Systems Journal*

Robert, M (1980) 'Market fragmentation versus market segmentation', *Journal of Business Strategy*, **65**, 3, pp 43–599

Rohlwink, A (1997) 'Treasury: A major growth area', *Banker*, April

Roth, K and Morrison, AJ (1992) 'Business-level competitive strategy: Contingency link to internationalization', *Journal of Management*, **18**, 3, pp 473–87, September

Schlesinger, LA and Balzer, RJ (1985) 'An alternative to buzzword management: The culture performance link', *Personnel*, September

Schmidt, J (1988) 'A case study: The strategic review', *Planning Review*, July/August

Stebbart, C (1985) 'Why we need a revolution on strategic planning', *Long Range Planning*, **18**, pp 68–766

Steiner, G (1986) *Strategic Planning*, Free Press

Sutton, GC (1980) *Economics and Corporate Strategic*, Cambridge University Press

Teall, HD (1992) 'Winning with strategic management control systems', *CMA Magazine* (RIA), March

Tita, MA and Allio, RJ (1984) '3M's strategy system: Planning in an innovative corporation', *Planning Review*, September

Tuller, LW (1991) *Going Global: New Opportunities for Growing Companies to Compete in World Markets*, Business One, Irwin

Vasconcellos e Sá, J (1989) 'Does your strategy pass the no test?', *European Management Journal*, **7**, 2

Vasconcellos e Sá, J (1989) 'A practical way to evaluate synergy' in *Handbook of*

Business Strategy, ed *Journal of Business Strategy*, Macmillan

Vasconcellos e Sá, J (1989) 'A theory of synergy', *Revue Economique et Sociale*, Université de Lausanne

Vasconcellos e Sá, J (1990) 'How to implement a strategy: A practical guide for the little rabbit', *Strategic Management Journal*

Vasconcellos e Sá, J (1991) 'Key success factors in marketing mature products', *Industrial Marketing Management*, November

Vasconcellos e Sá, J (1992) 'Macromarketing and Portugal: Problems and prospects', *Revista de Economia*, edited by Universidade Católica Portuguesa, **15**, 2, May

Vasconcellos e Sá, J and Amaral, MC (1993) 'Como Encontrar os Factores Críticos de Sucesso', Documento de trabalho 36/93, Instituto superior de Economia e Gestão, Universidade Técnica de Lisboa, April

Vasconcellos e Sá, J and Amaral, MC (1993) 'Como Estruturar uma Organização', Documento de trabalho 36/93, Instituto superior de Economia e Gestão, Universidade Técnica de Lisboa, April

Vasconcellos e Sá, J and Amaral, MC (1993) 'David Contra Golias', Cadernos de Económicas, Documento de trabalho nº33/93, Instituto Superior de Economia e Gestão, Universidade Técnica de Lisboa, March

Vasconcellos e Sá, J and Amaral, MC (1993) 'O Planeamento Estratégico numa Pequena Empresa: Simplificando o Processo', Cadernos de Económicas, Documento de trabalho 39/93, Instituto Superior de Economia e Gestão, Universidade Técnica de Lisboa, May

Vasconcellos e Sá, J and Amaral, MC (1993) 'O Planeamento Estratégico numa Pequena Empresa: Um Método Aplicado às suas Necessidades', Cadernos de Económicas, Documento de trabalho 39/93, Instituto Superior de Economia e Gestão, Universidade Técnica de Lisboa, May

Vasconcellos e Sá, J and Amaral, MC (1993) 'Uma Vez Mais Como Definir A Sua Missão: O Quadrado estratégico', Cadernos de Económicas, Documento de trabalho 33/93, Instituto Superior de Economia e Gestão, Universidade Técnica de Lisboa, March

Vasconcellos e Sá, J and Amaral, MC (1994) 'Guia de Planeamento Estratégico', Revista 'Exame', Year 6, **64**, June

Vasconcellos e Sá, J and Amaral, MC (1994) 'Manual para Fazer Publicidade', Revista 'Exame', Year 6, **71**, November

Vasconcellos e Sá, J and Amaral, MC (1994) 'O Estabelecimento de Objectivos para Implementar uma Estratégia: Uma aplicação Empresarial', Cadernos de Económicas, Documento de trabalho 3/94, Instituto Superior de Economia e Gestão , Universidade Técnica de Lisboa, March

Vasconcellos e Sá, J and Amaral, MC (1994) 'O Plano de Marketing numa Pequena Empresa (de Serviços de Engenharia)', Cadernos de Económicas, Documento de trabalho 2/94, Instituto Superior de Economia e Gestão, Universidade Técnica de Lisboa, January

Vasconcellos e Sá, J and Amaral, MC (1994) 'Os Deuses da Guerra' (Como Fazer um Plano Estratégico), Cadernos de Económicas, Documento de trabalho 9/94, Instituto Superior de Economia e Gestão, Universidade Técnica de Lisboa, October

Vasconcellos e Sá, J and Amaral, MC (1994) 'Plano de Estruturação de uma Empresa de Serviços de Engenharia', Cadernos de Económicas, Documento de trabalho 1/94, Instituto Superior de Economia e Gestão, Universidade Técnica de Lisboa, January

Vasconcellos e Sá, J and Amaral, MC (1995) 'As Tendências Estratégicas da Década de 90', Ensaios de Homenagem a Francisco Pereira de Moura, Edição do Instituto Superior de Economia e Gestão, Universidade Técnica de Lisboa, April

Vasconcellos e Sá, J and Miranda, MT (1993) 'Medindo o Conceito de Reorientação Estratégica', Cadernos de Económicas, Documento de trabalho 35/93, Instituto Superior de Economia e Gestão, Universidade Técnica de Lisboa, May

Vasconcellos e Sá, J and Miranda, MT (1993) 'Medindo a Estratégia', Cadernos de Económicas, Documento de trabalho 35/93, Instituto Superior de Economia e Gestão, Universidade Técnica de Lisboa, May

Venkatesan, R (1992) 'Strategic sourcing: To make or not to make', *Harvard Business Review*, November/December

Wilson, I (1992) 'Realizing the power of strategic vision', *Long Range Planning*, **25**, 5, pp 18–28, October

Index

The location of figures are shown in bold type.